MW01031590

"Dr. Jane Hamon doe
tians understand spirit.
Christian International ministry, we were going through some challenging situations. I challenged Jane to go behind the veil and discern what evil spirit had been assigned against us. She did and received the name of the spirit. We went into spiritual warfare, pulled that evil spirit down and destroyed it. Things changed for the better after that. She has done that several times for the ministry. Jane's writing makes spiritual discernment practical and real for everyone to receive and practice. Every Christian needs to read this book to increase their spiritual discernment and exercise the gift of discerning of spirits."

Bishop Bill Hamon, Christian International Apostolic
and Global Networks; author, *God's Weapons of War*,
Seventy Reasons for Speaking in Tongues and more

"I have witnessed firsthand the high level of discernment with which Jane Hamon operates. My wife and I, in fact, have been beneficiaries of her sensitivity. With great confidence, I can assure you that Jane's understanding and maturity in this area are unsurpassed. Thankfully, these insights are now in print. Read it!"

Dr. Dutch Sheets, Dutch Sheets Ministries

"Few people in the Body of Christ today have the depth of biblical teaching combined with revelatory insight as Jane Hamon. Her book *Discernment* proves my point! If you want to grow in knowledge coupled with supernatural gifting, then this book was written with you in mind!"

James W. Goll, founder, God Encounters Ministries;
author, *The Lifestyle of a Prophet*,
The Lifestyle of a Watchman and more;
recording artist and consultant

"This book, *Discernment*, will absolutely change your life. Jane Hamon has written an excellent analysis of this spiritual gift. She reveals details that will show you how to know what is behind the spiritual attacks you are encountering. Whether or not you personally have the gift of discernment, this book will set you free!"

Cindy Jacobs, Generals International

"As I sat and read *Discernment*, I recognized not only that this book was a word from Prophet Jane Hamon, but that God had given her a clear message to the Church in this hour. One of the greatest gifts God has given to His people is the gift of discernment. This book is a manual to help every believer and will give you tools necessary for proper discernment in the days ahead. With gross darkness all around us, it is imperative that we learn this most valuable gift from God. *Discernment* is an excellent book on the subject; you won't be able to put it down."

Charlie Shamp, author, *Mystical Prayer*;
president and founder, Destiny Encounters International;
www.destinyencounters.com

DISCERNMENT

DISCERNMENT

THE ESSENTIAL GUIDE TO HEARING THE VOICE OF GOD

JANE HAMON

Chosen

a division of Baker Publishing Group

Minneapolis, Minnesota

© 2019 by Jane A. Hamon

Published by Chosen Books
11400 Hampshire Avenue South
Bloomington, Minnesota 55438
www.chosenbooks.com

Chosen Books is a division of
Baker Publishing Group, Grand Rapids, Michigan

Printed in the United States of America

Library of Congress Cataloging-in-Publication Data
Names: Hamon, Jane, author.
Title: Discernment : the essential guide to hearing the voice of God / Jane Hamon.
Description: Minneapolis : Chosen Books, 2019. | Includes index.
Identifiers: LCCN 2019021620 | ISBN 9780800799557 (trade paperback) | ISBN 9781493421749 (ebook)
Subjects: LCSH: Discernment (Christian theology) | Discernment of spirits.
Classification: LCC BV4509.5 .H264 2019 | DDC 248.4—dc23
LC record available at https://lccn.loc.gov/2019021620

Cover design by Rob Williams, InsideOutCreativeArts

19 20 21 22 23 24 25   7 6 5 4 3 2 1

For Tom

You are such a gift to me! Thank you for all the support,
strength and wisdom you have given me as we have served
the Lord together. I am so blessed to be married to a man
who loves me unconditionally, loves God passionately
and encourages me to be strong and courageous in all
I do. I love doing life, family and ministry with you!

Serving Each Other,
Together Serving the Lord!

CONTENTS

Foreword by Dr. Chuck D. Pierce 11
Introduction 15

1. Hearing the Voice of God 25
2. Discerning the Times 43
3. The Issachar Anointing 59
4. Having a Discerning Heart 75
5. Discernment to Lead 87
6. Discernment to Build 101
7. Discerning the Spirit of God 115
8. Discerning Angels 129
9. Discerning Demons 145
10. Discerning the Human Heart 161
11. Discernment and Spiritual Warfare 181
12. Discernment and Intercession to Transform Territories 201
13. Discerning and Identifying Strongholds 221
14. Eyes to See, Ears to Hear 239

Index 243

FOREWORD

Once you are a child of God, you can be anointed by God. The enemy, however, longs to keep your spirit encased. In Hebrews 4:12 we find that "the word of God is living and powerful, and sharper than any two-edged sword, piercing even to the division of soul and spirit, and of joints and marrow, and is a discerner of the thoughts and intents of the heart." By living in communion with God and knowing His Word, we can actually increase in discernment. Discernment is a function in the intuition of our spirit. This is a time when we must discern that we are going to be victorious in the earth. *Discernment: The Essential Guide to Hearing the Voice of God* by Jane Hamon is a critical tool for the days ahead to help us maneuver strategically through the times that are on the horizon. Jane is like a sister to me, and I have been privileged to minister with her and her husband, Tom, throughout the last few decades. She is an incredible speaker, leader and author, and her newest book could not be more timely.

Training Our Senses

Every time I have received a vision of the future, the Lord has also spoken words that have given me courage.

11

"But, Lord, I do not have the ability to discern at this level," I have often said.

And each time, it was as if the Lord replied that I did not have a choice.

Discipline yourself in the Word and exercise My Spirit within your spirit, He would say, *for it will take both Word and Spirit to cause the reality of Me to be seen in the days ahead.*

If we quench the Holy Spirit in our lives, or if we do not wash ourselves with the written Word, we will fall out of spiritual balance and open ourselves to delusion. Under those conditions we will never reach the level of discernment we will need for the critical times ahead.

A dichotomy between good and evil is forming in almost every arena of life; there will be a fine line of division regarding how we discern. We must train our senses to discern good and evil. Hebrews 5:14 says, "Solid food belongs to those who are of full age, that is, those who by reason of use have their senses exercised to discern both good and evil."

We discern by the Word and the Spirit. That means for many of us that the Word of God must come alive again! This is my greatest concern for the generations that are arising. I do not see that the foundation of the Word has been built within them. The enemy will attempt, therefore, to counterfeit spiritual dynamics. We must know both Word and Spirit. I also see that those who have been involved in the cessationist philosophy (which says that God quit demonstrating His power centuries back) will have a difficult time in days ahead. There will be certain circumstances that we will be able to know, see and discern only by the Spirit.

The Discernment War!

Allow me to share a dream that one of my mentors, Lacelia Henderson, had many years ago. The dream has stuck with me through the years, probably because it seems more relevant now than ever!

In the dream I had gone with friends (Charles and Charlene) to a cabin they had in the woods. We were dressed for bed when someone knocked at the door. Charlene started to answer the door, and I waited in the bedroom. I said I would hide back there while she answered the door. If it was a friend I would come out, and if it was not I would jump out the window and run for help.

When she opened the door, men came in who were dressed in Army fatigues. They came in like the Gestapo and took the place by storm (captured it). In the meantime I had jumped out of the window in my nightgown. When they saw the open window they knew that I had escaped. Some of them ran outside and got in a vehicle (like a jeep) to look for me. It was very, very dark. I was alone and vulnerable (in my nightgown). Their eyes were piercing as they scanned to and fro, trying to spot me. When they were not looking my way I would run from tree to tree. It was all very intense, and I had little time to get behind the next tree before they looked back my way each time.

Finally, I came to a clearing and saw some houses. But I knew that I had to choose carefully which house to run to. It had to be someone who knew me and trusted me. I knew that once I stepped out into the clearing I would be spotted. I also knew that when I ran to a house to use the telephone to call for help, I would not have time to explain the situation in order to get permission to use the telephone. If I took time to explain, I would be caught and stopped by the enemy. Once I got to the house I had to be able to run straight to the phone to make the call for help.

This dream reveals to us the war ahead over discernment. We will have to know when to hide ourselves, when to come forth boldly with a word, when to run, when to fall, when to stand, when to make our way through a crowd, when to embrace revelation (and when not to!), when to be quiet and when to release the sound of the Lord loudly.

Discernment means that we will rightly divide the complexity of the events around us and choose the best way to advance. Discernment and faith work hand in hand. Continuous exercising of faith causes you to come to full age or maturity. You learn to divide between sound and unsound stimuli. This allows you to act with proper conduct and avoid misconduct on your path of life. You will hear a word from behind or recognize His voice inside of you. You must heed that call and obey.

Jane's book could not be a better resource to help you hear the voice of God. *Discernment* will help you develop a thought process and spiritual awareness that will cause you to walk in triumph in the days ahead.

Dr. Chuck D. Pierce, president, Global Spheres, Inc.; president, Glory of Zion International Ministries

INTRODUCTION

Have you ever been in a situation where everything looked right but felt wrong? Or have you ever met someone others admire and promote, yet about whom you have a deep sense of unease? Have you ever had a foreboding nightmare that you blamed on last night's pizza, but you cannot shake the feeling that God was trying to show you something important? Have you sensed the presence of angels or demons? Or have you ever been overwhelmed by the presence of the Lord and heard His voice at an unusual time or in an unusual setting?

As a prophetic person, I have learned that God loves to speak to us to help us navigate life with victory as we discern both His plans and the plans of darkness. His voice directs, comforts and empowers us and provides every necessary insight for us to accomplish our divine assignments, to confront dark powers and to live lives that are pleasing to Him.

For more than 35 years I have operated in discerning of spirits, which is one of the nine gifts of the Holy Spirit given to believers. As a young prophet, I received several prophetic words that indicated God had given me this gift as part of my prophetic gift mix; however, I never heard any specific teaching on the subject. I did not know anyone who operated fluently in this gift, or who could explain its dynamics or function, or who could teach me to activate it in such a way as to be a blessing to others. I lacked any kind of paradigm for what discernment actually is.

Sure, I would have a gut reaction to certain people and want to avoid them and know not to trust them. Or I would be in beautiful places that should evoke feelings of peace and security but, rather, caused me to experience internal distress due to a sense of darkness and danger. But I never thought of this as discerning the voice of God. On some occasions I saw demons manifest in my room but did not know this was discerning of spirits. In my earliest walk with God, I recognized the Spirit of God and His presence as I sensed, felt, heard and experienced His reality, but never did I realize that this was another aspect of discernment. On more than one occasion I knew angels were present to protect me, even seeing them intervene in dangerous situations, but I had no paradigm about the reality of the surrounding spirit realm.

There were no books on this specific subject to help me identify the things I was seeing and sensing. I found a few that discussed the nine gifts of the Holy Spirit, yet to me it seemed the sections about discernment were generalized or mystical.

My Journey Begins

In the late 1980s, our ministry, Christian International, was pioneering the prophetic movement and activating believers to hear the voice of the Lord. My husband, Tom, and I had started a church at our home base in Florida under the covering and direction of his father and mother, Bishop Bill and Evelyn "Mom" Hamon, along with other family members and friends. It was an exciting time as God began to emphasize the ministry office gift of the prophet. Believers were discovering that God did not speak solely to prophets and pastors, but that everyone could hear His voice. Our ministry led the way in what became a worldwide prophetic movement. Our church began to grow, as did our ministry staff.

During this time I met a person, whom I will call Jamie, who seemed to be gifted in many areas and attended prayer meetings and church services regularly. But there was something about Jamie that concerned me, that gave me an uncomfortable feeling. If asked, I could not have told you what it was that bothered me. Jamie had a warm smile and many friends, and seemed to love the Lord.

Then I learned that Jamie had announced plans to start a ministry and had convinced several others to join the endeavor. I saw an obvious ability to connect well with other people, but unfortunately, Jamie stole their hearts away by poisoning them with lies and suspicions about church leadership. I was right not to be trusting, and all my feelings were confirmed by Jamie's bad behavior.

In a confidential setting with Bishop Hamon and other team members, hoping to learn from the experience, I explained about the feelings I had whenever I encountered Jamie. I had no language for what I was sensing so I just blurted, "I never really liked or trusted Jamie! I felt this was a person who would do harm." (I have since learned that prophecy is not about what I am "feeling" on a soul level, but about the way God uses our souls to alert us to issues needing to be discerned.)

As Bishop Hamon asked me further about the experience, and why I had not expressed my concerns, I explained that I was raised with the saying "If you can't say something nice, don't say anything at all." I did not want to be guilty of being critical, judgmental or gossipy about someone else. So I said nothing. But God had given me discernment about what was happening so I could pray and perhaps help other people not be hurt or led away by Jamie's seduction.

Activation

That day, Bishop reminded me that I had received prophecies about having the gift of discernment. One of the prophetic words declared that God had anointed me as a watchman, saying that I would "see the snake and see the wolf." He suggested that the ministry leaders "lay hands" on me, a biblical practice described in 1 Timothy 4:14, and activate this gift fully so I could have eyes to see and ears to hear what I needed to discern for the Body of Christ—as well as for our ministry. So Bishop Hamon, my spiritual father and father-in-law, laid hands on me and activated that gift to another level of function. Within days I began to see, hear and sense more clearly demonic spirits that were present and operating around us. I heard conversations in the spirit realm. I saw impure motives and activities in people's lives that showed no visible signs in the natural realm.

To be honest, it was completely overwhelming and a bit unnerving. I love people! Generally I trust people. But sometimes I would hug someone at church and see or sense all kinds of dark or impure things. I did not like what I was experiencing—so I went back to Bishop Hamon and asked him to lay his hands on me again and take the gift back!

But rather than do that, he explained that gifts are given by the Holy Spirit to edify the Body of Christ. He challenged me to receive this gift of discernment as an aspect of the voice of God—a gift meant to be used as a blessing and a building tool for the Church. I would need to learn how to manage this gift with grace. He also encouraged me to remember that he and Tom would always help me walk in wisdom with what I heard and saw. I love leaders who are committed to bringing out the best in people!

Discerning Demonic Assignments

Not long after this, our ministry faced a number of difficult challenges. Finances began drying up; many people in our church suddenly faced bouts of discouragement; accidents were occurring; various sicknesses were spreading. In the midst of this, our team of intercessors began having dreams of spiritual warfare. It became apparent that we were undergoing a spiritual attack.

Finally, one morning, prayer partners from around the nation began calling to tell me that God was showing them the battle we were fighting. By noon I had received six phone calls from intercessors who all used similar words to describe the demonic assignment we were dealing with: oppression, deception, defrauding and division.

I took this information to Bishop Hamon. He challenged me to "go behind the veil in the spirit" and press in to see if the Lord would give me the specific name of this demonic assignment.

I looked at him in disbelief. "I don't know how to do that!" I said.

He told me basically that "going behind the veil" meant praying in tongues, stirring up the gift, activating the gift and listening. He said that when I followed these suggestions God would speak.

This sounded to me like an oversimplified statement of a complicated process. Besides, seeking the name of a demonic assignment seemed a little bit weird to me; I have never wanted to be weird or spooky spiritually. Nevertheless, I did as he asked—and God spoke very clearly to me.

Now, in case you have a picture in your mind of what "going behind the veil" might look like, I want to share the environment in which the Lord spoke. When I tell people about this, they usually ask: "Did you fast and pray for days? Did you shut yourself into your prayer closet with God for hours? Did you have an 'out of body' experience?" The short answer is no. Though those are all valid ways to press into the presence of the Lord to hear His voice, that is not what happened.

Instead, I was driving my three children and my neighbor's three children into town, a 45-minute ride, to do some shopping. I had six children under the age of six in my van, it was pouring down rain, and my windshield kept fogging up. While they listened to children's music, I began praying and asking God how this was going to work. How would I get the name of a demonic spirit?

Honestly, what I was saying was, "Lord, I am not sure I even believe in doing this. It seems kind of strange. But if You want to speak the name of this demonic spirit to me, I will listen." It was not a great prayer of faith and power!

Suddenly, I heard a name. I did not hear it audibly, but I heard it very clearly with my spiritual ears. It seemed strange. I had recently read a Christian novel, *This Present Darkness* by Frank Peretti, that had a plot regarding the activity of dark spiritual forces affecting a small town. What I was hearing seemed like a page out of one of his chapters. In my uncertainty I leaned forward and wrote the name I heard in the fog on my windshield and stared at it as I drove.

This is just strange, I thought. *How do I even know this is right?*

I decided to pull into a Christian bookstore and see if I could find any reference to this unusual name. With the six young children under tow, I walked into the store, pulled a Strong's concordance from the shelf and began to look up the word phonetically.

The name I heard was *Tokamene.* Strange, right? But when I looked it up I found a combination of two Hebrew words: *tok*, which means "injury, to oppress, to deceive, to divide and to defraud," and *mene*, which means "numbered" and comes from a root meaning "being assigned or appointed." God was telling me the name of the demon assigned to injure us, oppress us, deceive us, divide us and defraud us!

Quickly I loaded the kids back into the car, finished my errands and went home to discuss a strategy for prayer with Tom,

Bishop and other leaders. We took time that week to fast, pray and do spiritual warfare against this demonic assignment. We saw tangible results of breakthrough immediately.

One other note about this experience. Did we have to have the exact name of the spirit in order to break this assignment against us? I think not. But I can tell you that our faith was engaged knowing we were receiving from heaven the battle strategies and insight we needed.

Learning to Discern

In the beginning I made a lot of mistakes, not necessarily in what I was seeing or hearing but in keeping my heart right. It was easy to become judgmental and critical from what I was hearing God say. I had to learn to discern what came from my soul and what came from the Holy Spirit. I had to learn that sometimes my own opinions got involved and blocked me from seeing what was occurring in the spiritual realm or in the natural realm. Ephesians 1:17 speaks of having a spirit of revelation but also a spirit of wisdom. I had a lot to learn and great leaders around me to help me grow in grace and wisdom.

At times, I felt overwhelmed by what I was seeing or over-burdened by the responsibility of the revelations. What was I supposed to do with everything God was showing me? Many times I became frustrated and said or did the wrong thing. There were times when I simply wanted to ignore the gift or close my spiritual ears to the voice of God because I dreaded making a mistake on such important matters.

Others with the gift of discerning of spirits express similar challenges. Some shut down the operation of this gift in their lives because they grow frustrated with seeing things in the Spirit when they have no idea of what to do with that information. The internal pressure of receiving a flood of revelation without any strategy for its use is overwhelming. Others shut it down because they made mistakes with some of the information they received. Those bad experiences hurt people or led to misunderstandings with leaders in their churches.

It is imperative for people with discernment revelation to pursue the balancing anointing of wisdom that Paul spoke about when he prayed for the church at Ephesus. This was written to a first-century church planted right in the heart of a city that was the center of the known world for goddess worship, magic and occult training. If anyone needed discernment it was these believers. He wrote:

> [I pray] that the God of our Lord Jesus Christ, the Father of glory, may give to you the spirit of wisdom and revelation in the knowledge of Him, the eyes of your understanding being enlightened; . . . according to the working of His mighty power which He worked in Christ when He raised Him from the dead and seated Him at His right hand in the heavenly places, far above all principality and power and might and dominion, and every name that is named, not only in this age but also in that which is to come.
>
> Ephesians 1:17–21

The truth is, we are living in such critical times today that it is imperative for believers to learn to know the voice of God and be able to function in every tool given to us by the Holy Spirit. We are called to be Kingdom influencers—not only to discern angels and demons but also to discern the presence and power of the Holy Spirit, to discern the times in which we live and to prophesy His words as He directs us.

Spiritual discernment gives us a strategic advantage to win every battle. It releases divine intelligence from God's heavenly command center in order for us to identify our foe and overcome in this world. Our mission is to push back the gates of hell and advance the Kingdom of God. To accomplish this assignment, God has given every believer the supernatural ability to operate with "Holy Spirit radar" to see and sense things in the unseen realm. John 7:24 tells us to "look beneath the surface so you can judge correctly" (NLT). Hidden things are revealed so the Church can come to a greater place of authority, health and liberty; it is possible even for regions in the earth to be set free.

God is challenging His prophetic people—for, as we will see, we are all called to be prophetic—to be equipped with this exciting, multidimensional anointing for breakthrough. Spiritual discernment is not just about discerning demons and demonic strongholds, although it does offer a clear perspective on activity in the spirit realm. But it will also reveal strategies by which those strongholds are dismantled and destroyed. It will give insight for discerning angelic interactions with man and show how to respond to the movement of angel armies between heaven and earth. It will highlight hidden motives of the human soul that can deceive the unsuspecting and disrupt God's plan. Discernment, when coupled with wisdom, enables us to perceive the move of the Holy Spirit and align ourselves with His Kingdom purpose. This enables us to recognize and resist evil and be empowered to triumph in every spiritual battle.

Discernment is not a sideline issue with God but is the very manifestation of the counsel of the Holy Spirit in the life of the believer.

My prayer is that this book will shine the light of God's Word on the function and operation of this important gift of discernment in your life and bring you to a new dimension of discerning the voice of God. My heart is that God will allow my personal growth experiences to be of benefit to you in the sphere of our culture where God is equipping you to advance His Kingdom. The voice of the Lord brings life, freedom, hope and deliverance every time. May God's Spirit of wisdom and revelation empower you to have eyes to see and ears to hear what He is saying to His Church today.

1

HEARING THE VOICE OF GOD

The voice of the LORD is powerful.

Psalm 29:4

My husband, Tom, and I were attending a local Christian business leaders' meeting when I looked across the room and saw friends, a couple, who were successful real estate brokers. They were amazing! During the economic recession they managed to position themselves to prosper by listening to the voice of the Lord. While others had to close their businesses, they managed to grow and increase during one of the most difficult financial downturns of modern day.

I waved at them and suddenly heard the Lord say, *Go over there and break the spirit of robbery off their lives and business.*

To be honest, I actually argued with God!

Lord, really? A spirit of robbery? They seem so blessed and prosperous. They are an amazing example of how You bless even during hard times. . . .

I heard God respond to my argument: *Shhhh! Just go do it!*

I understood immediately that I did not have all the facts about what was going on in their lives—and He did.

So with a quick word to Tom, I walked over to them. After hugging and greeting them I explained what God had spoken to me. I was to break off a spirit of robbery.

They looked at one another and then responded to me. "Is that what is happening? Wow! We have been doing business for 35 years and God has always led us to prosper. But over the last five weeks everything has gone wrong. We have had issues with our staff, and with our family—and every time we have prepared to come to the closing table something has gone wrong, and we have lost the deal. As a matter of fact, we have lost almost five and a half million dollars of sales in the last five weeks."

I explained that God was revealing the source of their troubles. It was not because they were doing something wrong; it was because a spirit of robbery was resisting them. I said that we had the authority through the name of Jesus and the power of His Word to break off the demonic assignment. We prayed together, and I spoke aloud Exodus 22:7 (NIV) as a decree, which says, "The thief, if caught, must pay back double."

Six weeks after this conversation, the couple called to say that since our prayer they had finalized more than eleven million dollars' worth of sales, a double portion of what was stolen from them! God was faithful to His Word to restore double. Isaiah 61:7 (MESSAGE) says, "Because you got a double dose of trouble and more than your share of contempt, your inheritance in the land will be doubled and your joy go on forever." God gave them double for their trouble.

How did this breakthrough come? It came by hearing the voice of God as He provided insight and discernment in a situation I knew nothing about. His voice gives us answers from the supernatural realm that bring a tangible release of breakthrough in the natural realm.

My initial response of questioning what I heard from God is, sadly, the case of how we often limit ourselves by looking to the natural realm for what we see, hear and know. Discerning God's voice and the strategies of the enemy unlocks unlimited potential for believers to experience victory and freedom—and, like that couple, we can even expect a double-portion restoration of all that has been stolen by the "thief."

Jesus says, "The thief comes only in order to steal and kill and destroy. I came that they may have and enjoy life and have it in abundance (to the full, until it overflows)" (John 10:10 AMP). The Greek word for *abundant life* means "superabundant in quantity, superior in quality, exceedingly abundant above, beyond measure, more, more eminent, more remarkable, more excellent, more than necessary, super-added." Wow! This promise from God's Word encourages us with what we can expect when we hear the voice of God and discern the work of the thief, the source of our troubles.

. . . And They Shall Prophesy

Before I was in a position to receive clear discernment to help this couple, it was first necessary to lay a foundation in my life regarding hearing the voice of the Lord. I had spent most of my walk with God learning to tune my ear to His voice and to prophesy what I heard Him say. Prophecy sounds like a deep and complicated spiritual concept, but it merely means hearing what God says and speaking it out loud. When we prophesy and release the words of God, we are not speaking words of information for people to hear and process with their natural minds. Rather, we are declaring powerful, creative "God-words" of impartation that have the ability to shift spiritual atmospheres, release light and life and drive out darkness.

In Jesus' last words to His disciples before He ascended into heaven, He told them to go back to Jerusalem and wait for the promise of the Father, for "you will receive power when the Holy Spirit comes upon you" (Acts 1:8 NLT). The word *power* is the Greek word *dunamis*, which means "a force, miraculous power, a miracle itself, strength, worker of miracles." When we receive the power or force from the Holy Spirit within us, it gives us the ability not just to work miracles but also to live super-natural lifestyles, filled with His explosive might and strength.

Acts 2 then tells the story of the outpouring of the Holy Spirit upon those waiting in the Upper Room. Peter declared what was happening by quoting Joel 2:28–29:

> "And it shall come to pass in the last days, says God, that I will pour out of My Spirit on all flesh; your sons and your daughters shall prophesy, your young men shall see visions, your old men shall dream dreams. And on My menservants and on My maidservants I will pour out My Spirit in those days; and they shall prophesy."
>
> Acts 2:17–18

As we are filled with the Holy Spirit, we can all prophesy!

Prophecy, dreams and visions are part of the promise of the Father that Jesus gave His Church to fulfill our commission in the earth. We are told to desire to prophesy (see 1 Corinthians 14:39); that we can prophesy one by one (see 1 Corinthians 14:31); and that we are to desire spiritual gifts but especially that we may prophesy (see 1 Corinthians 14:1).

We are also taught that we can prophesy according to the proportion of our faith (see Romans 12:6), even though we know only in part and prophesy in part (see 1 Corinthians 13:9). First Corinthians 14:3–4 says that prophecy is for edification, exhortation and comfort, and it builds up the Church. Revelation 19:10 teaches us that "the testimony of Jesus is the spirit of prophecy." What a powerful gift God has given to us by the Holy Spirit to enable us to fulfill His Kingdom purposes in the earth!

The Voice of the Lord Is Powerful

God's voice is a force. His Word has the power to move im-movable circumstances and to transform situations. When we discern prophetically and then speak what God is revealing, that word has the power to heal, deliver and set free.

Scripture declares that "the voice of the LORD is powerful" (Psalm 29:4). The Hebrew word for *powerful* is *koakh*, which means "force, might, strength and wealth." When God speaks, things happen. Blockages are removed, hindrances are destroyed and blessings are released. Scripture also tells us that "the voice of the LORD will shatter Assyria [the enemy]" (Isaiah 30:31 NIV). Declaring what God says causes the powers of darkness to be crushed, and people and lands to be delivered. Jesus said, "The hour is coming, and now is, when the dead will hear the voice of the Son of God, and those who hear will live" (John 5:25). The voice of the Lord brings life.

So you see, hearing the voice of God is not a sideline issue in our Christian walk. Jesus said, "My sheep hear My voice, and I know them, and they follow Me" (John 10:27). It should be a regular part of the life of the believer to spend time not just praying to God but listening to Him as well, and cultivat-ing a prophetic lifestyle. Relationship with God means that we connect heart to heart with Him; we speak with Him and He speaks with us. God loves to speak and communicate with His people, revealing His will for our lives. He also wants to help us overcome the obstacles that block our destinies so we can establish His Kingdom in the earth. Every believer can and should learn to discern God's voice.

In his book *The Discerner* (Whitaker, 2017), James Goll explains it this way:

> Each of us needs to become a *discerner*—no matter what our personal background or specific gift function in the body of Christ. Although some believers are especially gifted as prophets, *every* follower of Jesus receives the gifts of revelation and discernment. And every believer needs to use them! . . .
>
> Developing discernment is not so much about knowing the future as it is about bringing the kingdom of God to bear on the time and place in which you live. . . . In a very real way, you and I bring God's Word to dwell in the midst of the world as we remain sensitive to the flow of His Spirit. Through our relationship with God, we receive revelation. And as we bring that revelation to the world around us, we actually incarnate His Word in our very ordinary lives.

Hearing and Obeying God's Voice

When God speaks, He wants us to be not only hearers but also doers of His word (see James 1:22). In *Spiritual Authority* (Christian Fellowship, 1972), Watchman Nee makes the point that "rather than being called believers it would be better if we were called obeyers." When God speaks He is looking for a response from His people. It could be a call to prayer, spiritual warfare, heart change or action. Hearing God's voice is one part; responding in obedience is another.

Deuteronomy 28 delineates the blessings that come from obeying the voice of the Lord. In this Old Covenant passage, we hear the heart of the Lord speaking to His people so that we can align ourselves and enjoy His blessings:

> "Now it shall come to pass, if you diligently obey the voice of the LORD your God, to observe carefully all His commandments which I command you today, that the LORD your God will set you high above all nations of the earth. And all these blessings

shall come upon you and overtake you, because you obey the voice of the LORD your God."

Deuteronomy 28:1–2

The chapter goes on to describe some of the blessings: being blessed in the city and the country; our children being blessed; the work of our hands and all our possessions being blessed. Our enemies will be defeated before our faces: "They shall come out against you one way and flee seven ways" (verse 7). Our bank accounts and workplaces will be blessed, as will our land. God will cause increase in all we do: "God will throw open the doors of his sky vaults and pour rain on your land on schedule and bless the work you take in hand" (verse 12 MESSAGE). We will be the lenders and not the borrowers, the head and not the tail, above and never beneath. The people of the earth will know that we belong to God and will hold us in respect.

We also know, of course, that the very next passage is a list of all the curses that come upon us for not obeying the voice of the Lord. Though we are under a New Covenant and know that Jesus became the curse for us, we also understand that doing things God's way will always bring a blessing, but doing things that are self-willed and disobedient will result in trouble. How much better is it for us to hear God's voice, discern His ways and obey?

Developing Our Spiritual Senses

The Bible teaches us that "solid food is for the mature, who because of practice have their senses trained to discern good and evil" (Hebrews 5:14 NASB). This means that our senses—both physical and spiritual—are vital to receiving revelation from God. It also means that discernment comes as our senses are trained. The more our senses are trained, the more discernment we will have.

When God created mankind, He instilled five senses into our bodies through which we receive information. Seeing, hearing, tasting, touching and smelling are the means we use to observe the world around us, to perceive our surroundings. This is how we keep ourselves safe and healthy.

God sometimes uses these physical, natural means to communicate with us, such as speaking in an audible voice within our hearing. He also speaks through the voices of prophets and prophetic people who have discerned His word, and we hear them with our physical ears.

But mostly God speaks to us through our spiritual senses. Did you realize that you are a spiritual being, that you will live eternally? You are a spirit, you have a soul, and you live in a body (see 1 Thessalonians 5:23). And we read in Job that "it is the spirit in man, the breath of the Almighty, that makes him understand" (Job 32:8 ESV). Our "spirit man" has its own set of senses.

When we come to Christ, God begins to develop these spiritual senses, enabling us to process spiritual information—and it begins with our natural senses. It is as we offer our natural senses to God and ask Him to utilize them to communicate with us that we begin to experience connection with heaven in a whole new way, and our spiritual senses are awakened. This is crucial to the discussion of discernment. Paul wrote this to the believers in Corinth: "The person without the Spirit does not accept the things that come from the Spirit of God but considers them foolishness, and cannot understand them because they are discerned only through the spirit" (1 Corinthians 2:14 NIV).

If God desires to show you something to help you understand a situation from a spiritual perspective, you most often will not see a large hand writing on a wall like in the days of Daniel, but you might see pictures or a dream with your spiritual eyes. You are rarely afforded a booming voice to announce God's directives, but you might hear with your spiritual ears.

When God spoke and told me to go to the couple and *break off a spirit of robbery*, I did not hear an audible voice that others in the room could hear; rather, I heard clearly through my spiritual ears. I have seen angels and demons at times through an "open vision," which involved my physical eyes, but most often I discern through the eyes of my spirit. I have smelled the beautiful fragrance of the Lord and at times the stench of a demonic presence, not only through my natural sense of smell but also through offering those senses to the Lord and being open for Him to communicate information to me through them. God will speak to us through our sense of taste as we are encouraged to taste and see that the Lord is good and believe that His word will be like honey on our lips (see Psalm 34:8; 119:103). There are times I feel a burning sensation in my hands, and I know God is present to heal. God loves to communicate with His people and delights in the creativity of activating all of our physical and spiritual senses for maximized connection.

My husband's uncle, Darrell Buck, has an amazing word of knowledge and healing gift. He often feels pain in an area of his body that he recognizes is not his own pain but rather God speaking to him through his sense of touch. If, for example, he feels a pain in his knee while he is ministering, he will ask if anyone is present who needs healing in his knee. There is always someone who responds. As soon as he prays, the pain lifts. He has had to learn to discern that the pain is not his pain; he has had to train himself to understand how God is communicating with him to describe the specific need to pray for.

In the verse from Hebrews quoted above, we are told to exercise our senses to discern between good and evil. This means we must be willing to activate our expectation for God to communicate to us through any of these means, spiritually or physically. If you are praying about a situation, stop speaking for a moment. Listen with your physical ears and look with your physical eyes—or be aware of taste, touch and smell—to see if God will use these physical means to download a spiritual answer to you. At the same time, realize that God might communicate a response to you through any of your spiritual senses as well.

In the natural, the more we exercise, the stronger and more proficient we become. It is the same in the Spirit. The more opportunity you take to focus on receiving from the Lord, the stronger and more proficient you will become. In this process you will learn to discern between your own voice and God's voice, as well as between your own imagination and the pictures, smells, tastes and touches that God is giving you.

Listening Intentionally, Hearing Intelligently

Psalm 85:8 says, "I will hear what God the LORD will speak, for He will speak peace to His people." The word *hear* is the Hebrew word *shama*, which means "to hear intelligently often with the implication of paying attention, to discern, to give ear, to listen, to obey, to make a proclamation." It has this connotation: "to listen intentionally and hear intelligently." In order to learn to discern God's voice, we must take time to stop and listen in an intentional way. This will give us intelligent answers to the questions we have.

As I was once praying about a miracle needed by one of my grandchildren, as well as for others in our church, I heard the Lord speak Psalm 85:8 as my answer. I was listening intentionally, and God spoke an intelligent strategy to me as to how to pray to see things shift. The verse says that God will speak peace to His people. This phrase *speak peace* in Hebrew is *dabar shalom. Dabar* means "to speak, to declare, to command with authority." *Shalom* is the Hebrew word for "peace, prosperity, favor, wholeness, health, wealth and rest." Someone said it carries the connotation of "nothing missing, nothing broken, nothing damaged."

So Tom and I began to decree the shalom power of God, *dabar shalom*, over our grandchild and other family and church members who needed miracles. One by one we saw God's miraculous hand move to heal bloodstreams, backs, joints and brains and do miracles beyond our imagination. God gave a strategy for prayer and healing because I took time to listen intentionally and hear intelligently.

Understanding Terms

The New Testament speaks of discerning of spirits as one of the nine gifts of the Holy Spirit. It addresses discerning the times, discerning good from evil and the need for believers to have spiritual discernment to process spiritual things. All these Greek words come from variations of the root Greek word *krino*, which means "to distinguish, to decide (mentally and judicially), to try, to judge." *Diakrisis* and *diakrino*, which refer to the gift of discerning of spirits, mean "to separate thoroughly, to make a distinction or a clear discrimination, to judge, to have perception, to have a sense of decision or judgment, to make a judicial estimation." When 1 Corinthians 2:13–16 speaks of things being spiritually discerned, the Greek word *anakrino* is used, which means "to separate or distinguish by looking throughout, to examine, scrutinize, question."

This is why it is so important for us to have a proper understanding of this gift from the Holy Spirit and how it is to function in our lives. The very definition uses words such as *judge*, *scrutinize* and *question*. God is not releasing this gift of discernment so that we walk with a critical and judgmental spirit, condemning people, seeing demons and being negative about the world we live in. No, He is releasing this gift so we can see the full picture of what is happening in the spirit realm and implement proper strategies in response—and also have a proper perspective on the natural world in which we live.

We must learn to question without being rebellious. We must learn to judge without becoming judgmental. We must learn to scrutinize without becoming critical.

The Cambridge dictionary defines the word *discern* as "to see, recognize or understand something that is not clear, to be able to decide something." The New Webster's dictionary defines *discern* as "to see or make out through any of the senses, to discriminate, to have insight and perception." Contained within this definition is the word *discriminate*, which means "to use good judgment in making a choice, to make distinctions."

Throughout this book I will use two terms for *discernment* interchangeably. I will use the word *discernment*, which refers to hearing God's voice, as well as the spiritual wisdom, understanding and perception that are received as we learn and grow through spiritual experiences and have our senses exercised to discern good and evil. I will also use *discerning of spirits*, which refers to supernatural spiritual insight of beings in the unseen realm, and which is received as a gift from the Holy Spirit.

I believe that everyone must operate in spiritual discernment, and that God has made the gift of discerning of spirits available to all. First Corinthians 12:31 tells us to covet the best gifts. Which is the best gift? It is the one needed to get the job done at the time. If someone needs healing, we access the gift of healing. If someone needs a word of prophecy, we hear the voice of God for prophecy. If we need discernment, we can access the gift of discerning of spirits to set captives free.

Using the gift of discernment involves operating in a prophetic dimension, and this is made available to every born-again believer. In the Old Testament only certain ones were appointed and gifted as prophets to hear God's voice and speak His purposes. Now, Acts 2 tells us that God is pouring out His Spirit on all flesh and every believer can receive revelation through prophecy, dreams and visions. Revelation is not reserved for an elite group; God is releasing the ability to hear His voice to an entire prophetic generation. This fulfills the declaration of Moses: "Oh, that all the LORD's people were prophets and that the LORD would put His Spirit upon them!" (Numbers 11:29).

We are now living in that day!

Natural Wisdom vs. Spiritual Discernment

First Corinthians 2:12–16 tells us this:

> Now we have received, not the spirit of the world, but the Spirit who is from God, that we might know the things that have been freely given to us by God. These things we also speak, not in words which man's wisdom teaches but which the Holy Spirit teaches, comparing spiritual things with spiritual. But the natural man does not receive the things of the Spirit of God, for they are foolishness to him; nor can he know them, because they are spiritually discerned. But he who is spiritual judges all things, yet he himself is rightly judged by no one. For "who has known the mind of the LORD that he may instruct Him?" But we have the mind of Christ.

In these words Paul explains that we cannot live a life of clarity and purpose merely out of human wisdom or reasoning, having our thoughts and perceptions shaped by culture or an unbiblical worldview. We must not be guilty of the same sin that Adam and Eve committed when God decreed they could eat of all the trees in the Garden except the Tree of the Knowledge of Good and Evil. They were the first people to fail to obey the voice of God because they did not discern the voice of the tempter. As a result, they embraced the lies of not just the devil but also their own human reasoning and decided for themselves what was right and wrong, partaking of the forbidden fruit. Scripture tells us that Eve was deceived (see 2 Corinthians 11:3). This caused her to fail to perceive or discern what was actually occurring and kept her from recognizing her enemy.

God has provided a gift of discernment to enable us to be sensitive to live Spirit-led lifestyles in which He speaks and reveals His thoughts, truths and directives. We align our lives accordingly, leaving the decision of what is right and wrong to Him. Spiritual things must be spiritually discerned. It is only by the Holy Spirit that we are able to judge between right and wrong, good and evil, His voice and any other voice. Hearing the voice of God is the basis for all discernment.

Eyes to See, Ears to Hear

We are the Body of Christ. Each one of us is a member or specific part of that Body and must learn to follow the directives that come from the head, which is Christ (see 1 Corinthians 12:7–12). My physical body responds to what my head says, and each one of my body parts has the responsibility to do its job for the function of the whole. Scripture paints the picture that each one of us has been created to function as a unique part of the Body of Christ and that we have gifts necessary to fulfill that specific membership ministry. To one is given the gift of prophecy, to another gifts of healing, to another the gift of discernment and so on.

In addition, whatever our particular giftings, when we are operating in the gift of discerning of spirits we become the eyes and the ears of the Body of Christ. We have the ability to see into the spirit realm and the natural realm in truth and reality. It gives us an element of operating with X-ray vision to be able to see things that the natural eye cannot see. Through the use of X-ray machines doctors can see hidden things, beyond what they see on the surface, and gain clarity regarding what is happening in a person's body in order to construct a strategy to bring the person to health. Discernment reveals hidden things in the realm of the spirit so the Body of Christ can come to a greater place of health, power, authority and anointing.

Paul gives us insight on this: "As it is written, 'Eye has not seen, nor ear heard, nor have entered into the heart of man the things which God has prepared for those who love Him.' But God has revealed them to us through His Spirit" (1 Corinthians 2:9–10).

In his book *Sparkling Gems from the Greek, Volume 2* (Harrison House, 2017), Rick Renner discusses this powerful word translated as "revealed":

> The word "revealed" is a translation of the Greek word *apokalupsis*, which is a compound of the words *apo* and *kalupsis*. The word *apo* means away, and the word *kalupsis* is the Greek word for a veil, a curtain, or some type of covering. When compounded, they form the word *apokalupsis*, which is normally translated in Scripture as the word revelation. This new word literally means to remove the veil or to remove the curtain so you can see what is on the other side. This word *apokalupsis* plainly refers to something that has been veiled or hidden for a long time and has suddenly become clear and visible to the mind or eye. It is the image of pulling the curtains out of the way so you can see what has always been just outside your window. The scene was always there for you to enjoy, but the curtains have blocked your ability to see the real picture. As soon as the curtains are drawn apart, you can suddenly see what has been hidden from your view. . . . So Paul was proclaiming in this verse that when the Spirit of God came to dwell within us, one of His major missions was to remove the veil that once obstructed our view. The moment you see beyond the curtain for the first time and observe what has been there all along that wasn't evident to you—that is what the Bible calls a "revelation."

So Paul was proclaiming in this verse that when the Spirit of God comes to dwell within us, one of His major missions is to remove the veil that once obstructed our view.

God is removing the veil from our lives, by the power of the Holy Spirit, so we can more clearly discern the hidden things and process them in the light of His love. God might bring an unveiling of revelation to us:

- Through the study of God's Word
- Through times of intimate prayer and worship
- Through Holy Spirit encounters
- Through revelation received in dreams and visions
- Through angelic or demonic interaction
- Through exploring impressions from the still, small voice upon our spirits
- Through God speaking through our natural five senses
- Through spiritually discerning natural world events in a biblical light
- Through spiritually discerning fulfillment of prophecy in Scripture
- Through exploring symbols or analogies inspired by the Spirit
- Through studying prophetic words released by other prophetic voices

God through His Holy Spirit is releasing a powerful, fresh dimension of the ability to discern the strategies of the enemy, the purposes and plans of heaven and its angel armies, and God's path forward to victory. Regardless of spiritual positioning or one's individual assignment from God, every believer needs to grow in the grace of the Lord to operate in discernment.

Leaders need eyes to see and ears to hear what the Spirit of the Lord is saying to the Church. Intercessors need insight into the realm of the spirit so they can pray strategically and wage successful spiritual warfare. Businesspeople and those called to government positions need the ability to separate, scrutinize and judge what is going on in the kingdoms of this world so as not to be deceived by the god of this world system and to operate above reproach as a Daniel or a Joseph. Ministry team members, counselors, cell group leaders and youth leaders need a well-developed gift of discernment to accomplish their assignments effectively. Every person who has any impact on a child's life needs discernment to navigate the complexities of helping that one grow in the faith. Students need discernment as they approach education in this modern age.

Every believer needs to hear God's voice in order to live a life of wisdom, victory and breakthrough every single day. As you ask God for discernment, He will be faithful to give you eyes to see and ears to hear what the Spirit of God is saying.

ACTIVATION

Take a moment to *shama*—listen intentionally and hear intelligently. Ask God to speak to you and tune your ear to the sound of His voice. He may give you a picture, a verse, a physical touch or a word. You may sense His presence, feel His power or smell His fragrance. Write down in your journal what you received.

2

DISCERNING THE TIMES

"Can you not discern this new day of destiny breaking forth around you? The early signs of my purposes and plans are bursting forth. The budding
vines of new life are now blooming everywhere. The
fragrance of their flowers whispers, 'There is change
in the air.' Arise, my love, my beautiful companion,
and run with me to the higher place. For now is the
time to arise and come away with me."

Song of Songs 2:13 TPT

We live in the panhandle of Florida just a few miles from
some of the world's most beautiful beaches. Our small
town is a resort community and vacation destination for millions. In the early 2000s we experienced an economic boom
as real estate was developed, and the people of our church
began to prosper. Most of them worked in real estate, con-
struction, banking, property appraisals and any other business
that dealt with land development and growth. Our church also

experienced prosperity as our members earned good livings and were faithful to give their tithes and offerings. We saw some of the largest offerings we had ever received during that period of time.

Rather than spend this money on the lists of projects and events we had in mind, we sensed God cautioning us to put all extra money aside and not to increase our budget by hiring more staff, doing major outreach or starting building projects. We discerned it was a time to store up, just as Joseph did in the times of plenty in Egypt.

After a couple of years of prospering and storing up, we heard the Lord say to us that we were coming into a time of "sifting in the shifting." I preached from Judges 7, the story of Gideon's three hundred who were anointed to win victories not by many but by few.

"The sword of the Lord and of Gideon!" we shouted with a great sense of anticipation of what was to come.

About six months later it seemed as though all hell had broken loose! Jobs were drying up. Money was no longer flowing. People began to leave our church to relocate to other areas for work.

I said to Tom, "What is going on? What is happening?"

He looked at me and said, "Honey, this is what you prophesied was going to happen. You said there would be a sifting in the shifting. Times have obviously shifted, and God made us ready for it."

I replied, "I had no idea it would look like this, though!" We obviously know in part and prophesy in part (see 1 Corinthians 13:9)!

Over the next several months the full force of the economic recession hit our community. All building and land development came to a screeching halt. Suddenly people were out of work. The first year almost sixty percent of our congregation was either out of work or experiencing a very difficult downturn.

More of our members left the area to find jobs. We were in a time of sifting as things were shifting, yet we held on to the promises of victory and overcoming God had given us for just that season.

As challenging as this was to navigate, we were financially prepared for something we could not have seen coming in the natural. We had properly discerned the word of the Lord to store up in time of plenty so that we would have resources for time of famine. Those were difficult years; however, our church did not have to lay off any employees and was never late in paying our payroll or our bills. We actually had money in the bank to help people who were struggling in the time of devastation.

We recognized that God had given us what is called the "Issachar anointing": a prophetic understanding of the times we were living in as well as the wisdom and strategy to know what to do in order to respond properly to what God was saying.

This is the "double portion" anointing that many speak of. It is both prophetic and apostolic. It is both the spirit of wisdom and the spirit of revelation. It is having a proper perspective about what is happening spiritually but also the wisdom to know how to respond to the natural circumstances of a new season.

Discerning the Signs of the Times

Jesus said this to the Pharisees and Sadducees who were trying to test Him:

> "When it is evening you say, 'It will be fair weather, for the sky is red'; and in the morning, 'It will be foul weather today, for the sky is red and threatening.' Hypocrites! You know how to discern the face of the sky, but you cannot discern the signs of the times [*kairos*]."

> Matthew 16:2–3

This was a rebuke from Jesus, urging the religious leaders not to judge matters merely by what they viewed with their natural eyes but rather to see with the eyes of the spirit and respond accordingly.

Today the Lord is challenging prophetic people to understand His times and seasons and align ourselves to them properly or we will miss the fullness of what God is doing in the earth and in the Church. When we know it is a time of urgency to press in in prayer and intercession, or perhaps a critical intersection in a cultural shift, or maybe a time to watch for divine connections and Kingdom opportunities, or even a time to move into rest, peace and prosperity, then we know how to respond. If the Lord says He will be doing a new thing, we must be careful not to allow religious mindsets of the past to cause us to resist a new paradigm.

Many prophetic voices today agree that we are in a key prophetic season as we enter the Third Great Awakening. The previous two periods of awakening were seasons of great revival breaking out in times of great darkness. We are living the words of Isaiah 60:1–3, which declares that in the midst of great darkness the glory of the Lord will rise upon His people and shine out to the nations. An awakening is an "epidemic revival." When an epidemic breaks out, almost everyone who is exposed to it catches and spreads it. We are coming into one of the greatest seasons of revival, reformation and divine visitation the earth has ever seen.

Shortly before His death, on approaching Jerusalem, Jesus spoke over the city, lamenting that the people of Israel had failed to recognize the day of His visitation (see Luke 19:41–44). Just think of that! The greatest move of God on planet earth in all of history was taking place among them, and the vast majority of the people of that time did not discern it. "He came to His own, and His own did not receive Him" (John 1:11).

This was a time like no other. This was not a time of looking forward to the day when God would send their Messiah to deliver them; this was actually the fullness of that time. Their Savior had come. And they missed it.

But those who did discern who Jesus was—Emmanuel, God with us in the flesh—and who believed in Him as Lord and Savior became sons of God and changed the world. God wants to give us eyes to see and ears to hear so that we can properly discern the times of the Lord.

So, does God have specific times and seasons when the truths of His Word become more evident and accessible than other times? Are there times of spiritual opportunity and anointing that God encourages us to partake of? Does God want to give us His perspective about what is going on in the earth so we can properly position ourselves and align with His purposes?

I believe the promises of God's Word can be accessed any time there is faith to receive what is written in Scripture. I also believe, however, that there are special moments when the heavens are opened to us and times of refreshing come from the presence of the Lord. But we must recognize them. We must embrace the new day of Kingdom purpose and rise to meet the Lord.

Understanding Time

Four Greek words referring to *time* appear in the New Testament, each having a specific meaning. We see these words used in some familiar passages of Scripture. Acts 1:7 (KJV), for example, states: "And he said unto them, It is not for you to know the times [*chronos*] or the seasons [*kairos*], which the Father hath put in his own power." To best understand what God is saying to us, we must understand His concepts of time and how they connect.

Aion

The word *aion* means "an age, eternity, everlasting, always, the beginning of the world, world without end." This is the word that is used to indicate the eternal nature of God who created time. Time was before the world began. It will be after the world comes to an end. This word indicates the concept of eternity. Hebrews 1:8 illustrates this: "Your throne, O God, is forever and ever; a scepter of righteousness is the scepter of Your kingdom." All other discussions of the concept of time fit within *aion*, for it is the eternal view of all that occurs.

Chronos

The word *chronos* means "space of time, season, chronological time, indication of delay." *Chronos* is the word used for the normal passing of time: days to weeks, weeks to months, months to years. *Chronos* can be translated "seasons," for the four seasons are a natural part of the passing of time. Galatians 4:4 speaks about God sending Christ to earth "when the fullness of time had come."

Chronos is what happens in our normal, daily course of life. Not every moment is marked by divine encounters or supernatural occurrences. Much of the time of our lives is passed in *chronos*, being faithful to the promises and principles of God, sowing and reaping, reading the Word, practicing devotion, paying bills, loving and caring for our families, and in general being diligent in our walks with God and people.

When time drags out, causing things to take a "long time," the word used is *chronos* (see Luke 20:9; John 5:6; Acts 8:1). For this reason one of the definitions of *chronos* is "indication of delay." When delay is happening there is a prolonging of the natural process of time.

Kairos

The word *kairos* means "a set time, an opportune time, an opportunity, a due season, a fixed or special occasion, the right time." *Kairos* is the word used when heaven and earth converge at an opportune time. Acts 17:26 (NIV) says that God has determined the "appointed times [*kairos*] in history." When *chronos* is prolonged or delayed, a *kairos* moment shifts everything. When a *kairos* moment comes, everything changes. It is the right time, the set time of God's favor. As a matter of fact, it indicates being in the right place at the right time for God-appointed results.

Peter used this word when preaching to his fellow Israelites:

> "Repent therefore and be converted, that your sins may be blotted out, so that times [*kairos*] of refreshing may come from the presence of the Lord, and that He may send Jesus Christ, who was preached to you before, whom heaven must receive until the times [*chronos*] of restoration of all things, which God has spoken by the mouth of all His holy prophets since the world began."
>
> Acts 3:19–21

When this passage speaks of times of refreshing, the Greek word for *refreshing* is *anapsyxis*, which means "a recovery of breath, revival." It comes from a root word that means "to cool off, to refresh oneself, to relieve, to recover from the effects of the heat."

God is promising us that as we come to Christ and have our sins blotted out, we can encounter Him in *kairos* moments that refresh and restore our souls and fill us with the breath of God. In the midst of the *chronos* of our day-to-day lives, praying, being faithful, sacrificing, obeying, He gives us *kairos* times of revival and a fresh breath from His Spirit.

These *kairos* moments are not limited to personal renewal; they also contain strategy that can cause a shift in a region or a nation. A revival or breakthrough in a region does not just happen. It occurs because we continue the normal course of walking with God and crying out for His presence on a consistent, regular basis [*chronos*]. Then God comes and gives us a "suddenly" season of outpouring, miracles and revival. He synchronizes the time and shows up to manifest Himself in a spectacular way. I think most of us have figured out that a "suddenly" experience does not really happen suddenly. Rather, after a long, diligent, *chronos* of preparation . . . then—suddenly—*kairos*! So you see *chronos* and *kairos* are connected.

Dutch Sheets, a dear friend and powerful prophetic voice to the Church, has an amazing grasp on the concept of time. In *God's Timing for Your Life* (Bethany, 2001) he helps us understand the connection between *chronos* and *kairos*:

> I have always separated the two concepts—chronological time and the right time—but God has been showing me that this is not accurate. Often they are simply different phases of the same process. *Kairos* in many ways is an extension or continuation of *chronos*. As the processes of God's plans unfold, *chronos* becomes *kairos*. . . . Life is a series of changes—a process of going from the old to the new—from *chronos* to *kairos*. Growth, change, revival—all are processes. Life is connected. Not understanding this, we tend to despise the *chronos* times of preparing, sowing, believing and persevering. . . . We are not losing or wasting time, we're investing it. And if we do so faithfully, the shift will come.

Hora

The word *hora* means "an hour, instant, season, high time, any definite time, point of time or moment." Romans 13:11 helps us understand that *kairos* and *hora* are connected: "Do this, knowing the time [*kairos*], that now it is high time [*hora*] to awake out of sleep." *Hora* is like *kairos* in that it indicates a specific point of time. *Hora* is the "now" time of God.

The word *now* is defined as "at the present time or moment, without further delay, immediately, at once." John 2:1–11 gives an account of the first miracle Jesus ever performed. He and

His disciples were attending a wedding when the host ran out of wine. Mary came to Jesus to ask Him to do something about this. He responded by saying, "My hour [*hora*] has not yet come."

But Mary, knowing who He was, reached into the *kairos* and, by faith, pulled it into the *hora* by putting a demand on the anointing she knew Christ had: "His mother said to the servants, 'Whatever He says to you, do it.'" Her faith shifted time and a miracle resulted.

Many times as Jesus ministered to individuals it was reported they were healed "in the same hour [*hora*]." This takes the *kairos* season of God and brings it down to a specific, identifiable point in time when things change. Jesus would often say to His disciples that "the hour is coming, and now is"—indicating not that things were going to shift, but that they had already shifted. When He spoke with the Samaritan woman at the well, He used this type of language: "The hour is coming, and now is, when the true worshipers will worship the Father in spirit and truth" (John 4:23). He was saying, "Things have shifted. Change is here."

Chuck Pierce, in his book *The Best Is Yet Ahead* (Wagner, 2001), gives us encouragement about how we can press toward our prophetic fulfillment:

> There are seasons in our lives that are now times—times of prophetic fulfillment when God's promises are manifested. In the natural cycle of life there are seasons. Some seasons are filled with desolation: but in those times we can take comfort in knowing that every season has a time frame. There is a time when desolation ends and prophetic fulfillment begins. . . . Daniel knew it was time for the word to be fulfilled and captivity to end. We, like Daniel, also need to come to a place where we understand God's time sequence. In my own life I know that when it is time for a desolation season to end, I want it done and its effects off of me. And once I get out of it, I don't

want to turn back. That's the attitude we need to have in moving forward into prophetic fulfillment. We need to be in close enough relationship to God so we know when to start into a new sequence and a new cycle of life. We need to know when it is time to cast off our desolation and move into a new season.

So in the overarching, eternal plan of God (*aion*), there is the normal passing of time (*chronos*), which if responded to properly sets us up for the opportune times of favor, breakthrough and refreshing (*kairos*). Within these *kairos* times are "now" moments (*hora*) for miracles. We must be sensitive to the Holy Spirit so we can shift our hearts and minds and align with our "now" seasons.

A Prophetic Word and Time

One year the panhandle of Florida was under a terrible drought. It had been months since we had any measurable rainfall in a climate that is usually quite humid and wet. Forest fires were breaking out around our property and the water table was getting low. The Weather Channel reported that we were in a "catastrophic drought."

Our church and ministry were preparing for our annual gathering of apostles and prophets, and I was asking the Lord if He had any specific prophetic assignments for me to release during the conference.

He said, *Yes, I want you to announce that I am bringing My people into the time of drought-breaking rain. You will see drought broken, for I will send a drought-breaking rain this week as you gather. First the drought will break in the natural, then it will break in the spirit as well.*

I hope you caught that. God was saying He would send a drought-breaking rain that very week! It was already Tuesday, and I knew that weather forecasters were saying there was no rain in sight. But I knew God's voice, so that night I prophesied what God said.

After the service Tom and I went home and tuned our TV to the Weather Channel. The meteorologists reported on the drought then made this statement: "This is a serious drought, and there is no rain in sight." I had just spoken a prophecy that God would send drought-breaking rain that week because it was time for the drought to end, yet the natural had not yet caught up with the spiritual.

We pointed our fingers at the television and declared, "It's going to rain!"

The next afternoon we came home and turned on the Weather Channel to get an update. This time they had a different report. They said there had been a "slight shift" in the atmosphere; we now had a very slim possibility of getting some rain. When they said *slight shift* I thought of Elijah declaring, "There is the sound of abundance of rain," yet it took a while before there was even "a cloud, as small as a man's hand."

That night after the service we again checked with the Weather Channel to see how the shift was progressing. They said, "Panhandle of Florida, we have good news! It looks as though you are going to get some rain tomorrow! But don't get too excited. This is not drought-breaking rain." Just a little more than 24 hours earlier I had prophesied that God would send a drought-breaking rain, but our friends at the Weather Channel were speaking the opposite. Tom and I once again declared the arrival of the new season of God with drought-breaking rain to come that week.

Thursday morning we awakened to the sound of rain. It rained that day. And it rained, and it rained, and it rained. We ended up with 21 inches of rain in a 24-hour period, which would cause flooding in most places. But here in sandy Florida the ground soaked up the water, filled our water table and suddenly ended our drought! On Saturday morning we got our local paper. A headline declared: "Drought-Breaking Rain Soaks the Panhandle of Florida."

This was not the normal passage of *chronos* between drought and rain. Nor was it only a *kairos* when God broke through to end the season of drought with a new season of plenty. This was a miracle of "now," *hora*, rain on the way. The *hora* of rain marked the new *kairos* season as a sign. God sent the rain just as He said He would, signifying the new season—not just in the natural but also in the spirit.

That experience gave us fresh faith to press in and believe for things that had been dry and delayed for a long time. Times of worship yielded amazing experiences in the tangible presence of the Lord. Healing and miracles began to occur with greater frequency. People started experiencing soaring faith and expectation as their families were healed, prodigals began coming home and doors of financial opportunity opened to many. In the same way, if God has given you a promise, He also has a *kairos* word that will shift the drought situation in your life to bring you into your personal times of refreshing.

Waiting for the *Kairos*

Time can be one of the most frustrating parts of walking out our prophetic promises. Joseph had prophetic dreams from God, but it took a long and painful thirteen-year process before he saw the dreams come to pass. David received a prophecy that he would be king, but again it took thirteen years of leadership training, betrayal and character development before he received the crown.

Abraham had a promise from God that he had nations in his loins and that God would give him and Sarah a son. But it took 25 years to see that promise come to pass. God waited until it was truly impossible to happen in the natural because Abraham was one hundred years old and Sarah was ninety. During the *chronos* time that passed, Abraham and Sarah decided to help God along and hurry the process, hoping to push *chronos* into *kairos*. As a result, Ishmael was produced, and he has troubled Israel to this day. Abraham was the father of our faith, so how could this happen? The Bible never says that Abraham ran out of faith but rather indicates that he ran out of patience.

What happens if you are in a *chronos* season of waiting for a promise to come to pass? It is important to remember that there were many *kairos* moments when Abraham encountered the Lord during his *chronos* period of waiting for the promise to be fulfilled. When we look at the lives of the patriarchs, often the recorded times in Scripture are *kairos* experiences that are marked with excitement and great change. But the *chronos* is often seen in the recorded gaps of time that still required great faith, patience and faithfulness.

In this manner, the writer of Hebrews encourages us to stay patient in the process:

> Therefore do not cast away your confidence, which has great reward. For you have need of endurance [which means cheerful or hopeful endurance, patience, constancy, steadfastness], so that after you have done the will of God, you may receive the promise.
>
> Hebrews 10:35–36

Dealing with the Spirit of Delay

There are many times when the promise of God is delayed because God is developing our character and preparing us for what is ahead. Joseph was prepared in leadership, government and knowledge of agriculture during his time of patience in the promise. But at other times the promise is delayed because the enemy is resisting our forward movement, throwing up barriers and blockages to the blessing and fulfillment God has for us. There are times when a demonic spirit of delay can be an assignment against the destiny of God in our lives.

A number of years ago Tom had a dream in which he saw a smooth-talking businessman speaking to a group of people, telling them of a "get rich quick" scheme. The room was filled with believers who were being drawn in and seduced into going off course from God's plan for them. When the man left the room, Tom asked the woman in charge what the man's name was. She replied that she did not know.

He said, "Ask him his name. He has to tell you his name."

When the man returned she asked him his name. He just smiled. She then demanded to know his name.

He said, "I am called by many names. Some call me Chronos; others call me Beelzebub; others just call me Pride."

As previously mentioned, one of the meanings for the word *chronos* is "indication of delay." The demonic assignment revealed in this dream was an attempt to lead people astray during their *chronos* times and get them out of alignment with God. He was the personification of a spirit of delay.

Interestingly, as I studied this I found references to a Greek demon god named Cronos (different spelling) who was known as the god of the harvest who controlled wealth, and also as the god of chaos and disorder. We should be aware that the enemy will often offer a promise of wealth, wrong opportunities or promotion in an attempt to deceive believers into abandoning their time of waiting on God and His true promises. This enemy will seek to create disorder in our lives, getting us out of the timing of God.

In the dream this spirit of delay was linked to Beelzebub and pride as well. Beelzebub was a New Testament type of Baal. His name meant "lord of the flies." Flies are a symbol of harassment and death. Pride refers to Leviathan, who was known as "king over all the children of pride" (Job 41:34). Leviathan always resists the process of God as well as the move of God when it arrives.

The spirit of delay will test the righteous and often cause trouble for those who fail to discern the times they are in. Some of the effects of yielding to the power of the spirit of delay are: passivity and spiritual slumber (see Matthew 25:5); misconduct among believers (see 1 Timothy 3:14–15); missed opportunity for advancement (see Numbers 13); disobedience and usurping of authority (see 1 Samuel 13:6–14); and idolatry (see Exodus 32:1).

Breaking Out of Delay

It is time to break out of delay and receive the fullness of promise. If you have fallen into any of the above bad behavior patterns as a result of delay, it is important to repent and turn away from sin and turn back to God, who holds time in His hands. When we align our hearts, God is faithful to synchronize our *chronos* and *kairos* to fulfill His purposes.

When we fail to discern the times of the Lord, we lose sight of the vision God has given us and experience trouble and missed opportunity as a result of our lack of alignment. Scripture is clear that those who wait on God are blessed, prospered and strengthened—if we do not lose hope in the process! We can remain in a place of peace and purpose even during a *chronos* season while we wait and press forward for our *kairos* and *hora* moments of destiny. If we truly discern the time we are in, we will know how to be aligned.

ACTIVATION

What time are you in? How are you positioning yourself to move into your "suddenly" season?

3

THE ISSACHAR
ANOINTING

The children of Issachar . . . had understanding of
the times, to know what Israel ought to do.

1 Chronicles 12:32 KJV

The Issachar anointing is having the ability to discern and
identify spiritual times and seasons and know how to respond. This was a central part of the gifting and function of
that particular tribe of Israel. As a prophet I find there are times
when the thrust of the prophetic word through me is focused
not only on understanding what God is saying to the Church,
but also on identifying the current spiritual season. This is a
function of the Issachar anointing that we all, as prophetic
people, should learn to operate in.

59

A Tipping-Point Moment

In January 2011 I preached several messages about overcoming the "spirit of Egypt." I felt there was something stirring in the earth that was signifying a time when people would cry out for deliverance and change, the way Israel did after four hundred years of Egyptian bondage. I used the word *Egypt* to represent the oppressive world systems that keep the people of God, and even nations, in captivity. These systems are under the control of the god of this world and resist the cry of the Holy Spirit to "Let My people go!"

During this time, when I joined a group for pre-service prayer, I heard the Lord say that we were entering a "tipping-point moment" in history. Individuals, churches and even nations were facing a critical time in which things could tip in the direction of good or evil depending on how we pressed in in prayer. There was obviously a new season emerging in the earth.

Webster's dictionary defines *tipping point* as "the critical point in a situation, process or system beyond which a significant and often unstoppable effect or change takes place." Wiktionary defines it as "the point at which a slow, reversible change becomes irreversible, often with dramatic consequences." The Free Dictionary defines *tipping point* as "a critical or pivotal point in a situation or process at which some small or singular influence acts as a catalyst for a broader, more dramatic or irreversible change." In his book *The Tipping Point* (Back Bay, 2002), Malcolm Gladwell defines it as "that magic moment when an idea, trend, or social behavior crosses a threshold, tips, and spreads like wildfire."

We see then that the tipping point is the moment at which something becomes irreversible and unstoppable. Momentum builds, often slowly and quietly, until it becomes impossible to go back to a previous state. It is a critical juncture in time, a defining moment in a series of events.

Within two weeks of that morning prayer time, northern Africa, Egypt and the Middle East broke out in revolution that came to be known as the Arab Spring. Headlines in the papers read: "Egypt at a Tipping Point." Newscasters used the phrase *tipping point* daily to describe the unrest that was taking place in that part of the world. Nations were hanging in the balance and could fall into greater darkness or into a new season of freedom. During the years immediately following the Arab Spring, it seemed as though these nations actually went into greater chaos. The rise of ISIS and the Muslim Brotherhood, the fall of Libya and later the overthrow in Turkey caused that area of the world to continue to destabilize.

Even in America we saw greater darkness encroach upon our society as morality declined even further, perversity was celebrated and religious persecution was on the rise. But in the midst of darkness, a light of reformation and spiritual revolution began to shine from God's people. As I noted earlier, we are living in days described by the prophet Isaiah:

"Arise, shine; for your light has come, and the glory of the LORD has risen upon you. For behold, darkness will cover the earth and deep darkness the peoples; but the LORD will rise upon you and His glory will appear upon you. Nations will come to your light, and kings to the brightness of your rising."

Isaiah 60:1–3 NASB

Yes, just as these words foretold the coming of the Messiah, we see, in the midst of darkness in our world today, their application to the light of God's glory shining brighter and brighter through His glorious Church. It is the season when the impossible becomes possible!

A friend explained *tipping point* to me this way. He said if several people decide they want to lift and tip over a heavy object such as a vehicle, they would get under it, lift, then shift and push until that vehicle hits a tipping point. At the tipping point there is a risk that the pull of gravity will cause the vehicle to fall back on top of them if they do not push hard enough. But if they push and it tips, the gravity that has been working against them now begins to work for them.

That is what happens with a spiritual tipping point. We lift through *prayer*. We shift and push through *prophecy* and *decrees* until suddenly all that has been working against us begins to work for us. The curse is turned to a blessing (see Deuteronomy 23:5)!

As believers we must operate in the Issachar anointing to recognize and cooperate with God's tipping-point moments in our own lives. There are times we must push through praying, prophesying and decreeing God's breakthrough for our families, our finances and even our physical health. As intercessors, as well, the anointing of the sons of Issachar is vital to discern the times and to know what to do as we push through and battle for the souls of nations.

Who Was Issachar?

Issachar was the ninth son of Jacob and patriarch of one of the twelve tribes of Israel. The sons of Issachar were known as valiant men who stood with their brothers in war (see Judges 5:15; 1 Chronicles 7:5). We learn from Talmudic writings and Jewish scholars that they were considered to be experts in the Law. This tribe of scholars studied the Torah intently and could advise leaders about what the Word of God had to say regarding particular issues and about going into battle.

They were also known as keepers of the Hebraic calendar, for they charted the movements of celestial bodies to observe the times for the holy feast days. One of their tribal standards has the image of the sun, moon and stars, an indicator of the anointing of Issachar. Though they studied the movements of the heavenly bodies, they were not sorcerers or astrologists who charted the stars for occult practices (see Deuteronomy 18:14); rather they interpreted the signs in the heavens as designed by God (see Genesis 1:14; Acts 2:19).

Anointed for Prophetic Discernment

Most famously the tribe of Issachar "had understanding of the times, to know what Israel ought to do" (1 Chronicles 12:32). The words *understand* and *know* are both the Hebrew word *yada*. *Yada* means "to know, to perceive, to discern, to distinguish, to discriminate, to be cunning, to advise, to have wit, to know by experience, to be skillful in, to be wise." This was not merely book knowledge but also personal understanding and prophetic revelation that were applied experientially. They had the power, as a unique breed of prophetic people in Israel, to see and know.

Not only did they see and know what was coming, but they also discerned strategies for how Israel was to position herself to receive a blessing. So many times I hear prophetic words being released that indicate a new time or season in God; however, if we fail to come into agreement with the declaration and never align our lives to receive from God, that season could pass us by without benefiting us.

Here is an example. Cindy Jacobs is a dear friend of our family and ministry, and is widely known for having a strong Issachar prophetic anointing on her life. She prophesied during one of our conferences that God was going to bring our local area into a time of prosperity and that real estate prices would skyrocket.

Tom and I had lived in our area for fifteen years and real estate prices had gone up a bit but nothing to be described as skyrocketing. At the time of this prophetic word we were struggling to make ends meet and were slow to respond. We had never done any investing of that sort, so we took a good deal of time investigating and learning about the market, and trying to figure out where the money would come from for us to invest.

But others who had more knowledge and faith responded immediately by buying investment property. Within the year, many people experienced their land values exploding up to fifty times the amount they paid! Tom and I had prayed about the idea of a new season, made decrees accepting the new prosperity and investigated the topic, but we never put ourselves into a position to partake of it. Remember, I told you I would share our learning experiences with you. Well, this was one big experience to learn from!

Whenever God speaks about a new season, we must be diligent to ask Him what we need to do to align with it. It takes discernment to see the new, but it also takes discernment to see the old we must let go of in order to embrace change. It takes prophetic eyes to see the new begin to form before it even exists. Abraham believed that God "calls those things which do not exist as though they did" (Romans 4:17). When we live with the eyes of Issachar we unlock hidden potential for miracles in the new season.

Anointed for Leadership

The sons of Issachar were known throughout Israel's history as those who were able to discern a shift of seasons; this included new seasons of leadership. One of Issachar's descendants, Tola, became a judge, and as a leader "he arose to save Israel" (Judges 10:1–2). The "princes of Issachar" worked with Deborah, the only woman judge named in the book of Judges (Judges 5:15), and served as warriors and advisers in God's campaign of freedom for His people. Issachar stood with David during a time of kingdom transition, though David was not from the current king's lineage. They were not afraid to stand with God's true leaders during times of change.

Our friend Chuck Pierce is a prophet and one of the strongest Issachar leaders in the Body of Christ today. He discerned times when our nation was coming into war, economic recession, destructive weather patterns and many other important seasons. He has given key words to our local church about our times and seasons of great change. In an Elijah List article (January 24, 2010) Chuck had this to say about Issachar's role in the time of transitioning from Egypt's bondage to Canaan's promise:

> Each tribe of Israel had a redemptive blessing. When God brought this people out of slavery in Egypt to move toward the promised land, He brought them out by armies. Each tribe was a warring army with a redemptive gift. Without each tribe warring for their portion, the full plan of God for the land, called Israel, could not be fully manifested in the earth. They moved toward their promise as the trumpet sounded and His presence, which was central, shifted them toward their destiny. Three of the twelve tribes moved together. Judah, the apostolic warring leadership tribe who understood sound, moved first. Then came Issachar, the Torah tribe, who would bear the burden for victory and wages. This tribe understood time and could interpret the Word of God in time. They were connected to Zebulun, the wealth tribe, because provision for the journey and the supply for victory were important.

Issachar's leadership style was not to proceed alone; in many places in Scripture you see Issachar standing with other tribes for Kingdom purposes. We must recognize that we need each other and that each of our gifts rises to a greater level of power when we walk together.

Anointed for Alignment

Moses spoke prophetically about the tribes of Zebulon and Issachar, saying, "They shall call the peoples to the mountain; there they shall offer sacrifices of righteousness" (Deuteronomy

33:19). Mountains were the high places of both true and pagan worship. The tribe of Issachar, as scholars of the Torah, was known as wise men who would align the people to the true place of worship and away from idolatrous altars. They brought alignment with righteousness through their knowledge of God's Law. The sons of Issachar aligned with David, even before he was anointed king, as they discerned that the time of Saul was over and a new time for the kingdom of Israel had dawned. Because they were scholars, all Israel looked to them to discern the times and to know what to do, especially in times of transition. They also joined in times of reformation, such as standing with other tribes as Hezekiah worked to restore Temple worship in Judah.

Today God is raising up a new generation of anointed leaders who have reformation and restoration in their hearts. They are able to discern moves of God and are sensitive to times of change. They are not constrained by the structures of old, dead religion, which has a form of godliness but denies its power (see 2 Timothy 3:5). They love the Word of God and are unwilling to compromise it to appease the culture of the day. The Issachar anointing empowers believers with spiritual intelligence to understand both the *logos*, the written Word of God, as well as the *rhema*, the Holy Spirit–inspired prophetic word of God.

My father-in-law, Bishop Hamon, has operated as an Issachar prophet for decades, identifying the modern restoration moves of God in advance so the Church can know the times and know how to align herself. In the 1980s he prophesied a coming prophetic movement, which was birthed worldwide in 1988. In the 1990s he began to prophesy about a coming restoration of apostles; an apostolic movement came into focus in 1998. In 2007 and 2008 he prophesied a saint's movement and announced the beginning of the third reformation of the Church. Many leaders worldwide have recognized this time period as a new era of the Kingdom of God in the earth. Bishop Hamon has been an Issachar reformation general helping the Church align with and shift into her new day.

Anointed for Intercession

Before Jacob died he blessed each of his sons prophetically and imparted understanding about the anointing on each one's progeny. He prophesied this about Issachar: "Issachar is a strong donkey, lying down between two burdens; he saw that rest was good, and that the land was pleasant; and bowed his shoulder to bear a burden, and became a band of slaves" (Genesis 49:14–15).

This picture does not suggest glamour—calling someone a donkey. It is a rather peculiar looking animal and spends its life working hard carrying the burdens of others. But in truth the donkey is a special animal in Scripture. It is a picture of those called to bear burdens in the spirit as watchmen and intercessors. It is a symbol of intercession, strength and humility.

Issachar intercessors are not lifted up in pride but remain humble in the midst of their strength. They are hard workers, willingly bowing their shoulders to bear the burden. Jesus encouraged us regarding how we are to bear burdens when He said,

> "Come to Me, all you who labor and are heavy laden, and I will give you rest. Take My yoke upon you and learn from Me, for I am gentle and lowly in heart, and you will find rest for your souls. For My yoke is easy and My burden is light."
>
> Matthew 11:28–30

We see in Numbers 22:21–34 a picture of an Issachar intercessor—the story of Balaam's donkey, who had more discernment than the supposed prophet and who spoke out loud to Balaam about the angel standing in their path. Issachar intercessors see clearly into the spirit realm and speak warnings that align with God's plans and purposes.

Issachar intercessors have an anointing for war. You may not see a warrior charging to battle on the back of a donkey, but Samson used the jawbone of a donkey to slay one thousand Philistines (see Judges 15:15–16). The mouths of Issachar intercessors have the power to slay many enemies as they wield the sword of the Word of the Lord and grasp His decrees as their weapons.

Two of the most familiar pictures of donkeys in Scripture show them present at the very beginning of Jesus' life as well as at the very end. The first picture we have is one we imagine of a very pregnant Mary riding on a donkey on the way to Bethlehem, preparing to give birth to the Savior of the world. The second is the picture of Jesus riding on the back of a donkey for His triumphal entry into Jerusalem to the sounds of loud *Hosannas*. This was a fulfillment of the prophecy in Zechariah 9:9 about the coming of a king, righteous and victorious, riding humbly on a donkey. Why a donkey and not a regal horse? Because horses were used by kings; donkeys were used by the common man. Jesus is King, but He came identifying with the common man. Jesus, like the donkey, humbly carried a burden, that of man's sin.

God is calling a generation of Issachar intercessors who are willing to bear the burden of the Lord to prepare the way for His return. Yes, they will be prophetic, with keen vision of the spirit realm and the ability to discern the times, but they will also be humble, hardworking "Christ-bearers," who usher in the presence of the Lord. They will live their lives with a heart of servitude to the call of God to intercede until the job is done.

Anointed for Prosperity

When the Israelites were coming out of Egyptian bondage God organized them into warring tribes according to their family lines. Each had a redemptive gift that would be used to possess the Promised Land and drive out the enemy Canaanite nations. Moses also spoke prophetically regarding each tribe. Regarding Issachar he said,

> "Rejoice, Zebulun, in your going out, and Issachar in your tents! They shall call the peoples to the mountain; they shall offer sacrifices of righteousness; for they shall partake of the abundance of the seas and of treasures hidden in the sand."
>
> Deuteronomy 33:18–19

This was a blessing of righteousness and prosperity. In this blessing Zebulun and Issachar were connected, speaking of the ability to form partnerships for prosperity. Remember, Issachar was a hardworking tribe. They would hire themselves out to work for other tribes in order to earn wealth. Issachar was anointed to "partake of the abundance of the seas and of treasures hidden in the sand." They were blessed by the sea and by the land. They had the ability to uncover hidden wealth, much like Cyrus, to whom God said, "I will give you the treasures of darkness and hidden riches of secret places" (Isaiah 45:3). Issachar has eyes to see opportunities in the *kairos* times of God for finances and resources to flow through their hands.

The Issachar anointing will cause us to prosper to become Kingdom financiers. Issachar is generous and full of favor. We will not only be blessed, but will be blessed to be a blessing.

Anointed for Rewards

To fully understand the meaning of Issachar's name one must first look to his conception and birth by his mother, Leah. Leah had already given birth to four sons for Jacob, and Rachel had yet to bear one. Yet Jacob loved and favored Rachel, her beautiful younger sister, above her. Leah was heartbroken, rejected, constantly competing with her sister. Leah believed that if she could find her worth in bearing sons, her husband just might come to love her. With a heart desperate for love she struck a deal with Rachel:

> Now Reuben went in the days of wheat harvest and found mandrakes in the field, and brought them to his mother Leah. Then Rachel said to Leah, "Please give me some of your son's mandrakes."
>
> But she said to her, "Is it a small matter that you have taken away my husband? Would you take away my son's mandrakes also?"
>
> And Rachel said, "Therefore he will lie with you tonight for your son's mandrakes."
>
> When Jacob came out of the field in the evening, Leah went out to meet him and said, "You must come in to me, for I have surely hired you with my son's mandrakes." And he lay with her that night.
>
> And God listened to Leah, and she conceived and bore Jacob a fifth son. Leah said, "God has given me my wages, because I have given my maid to my husband." So she called his name Issachar.
>
> Genesis 30:14–19

Mandrakes were known as "love apples" and were thought to possess powers of fertility. Rachel, who was barren, made a sacrifice of intimate time with her husband in order to obtain the mandrakes in hopes of conceiving a child in the future. Leah sacrificed her son's gift to her in order to have intimacy with her husband in hopes of winning his heart. There was much pain and sacrifice on both sides of this equation, much desperation for intimacy and fulfillment.

When Leah conceived and gave birth to her son she named him Issachar, which means "he will bring a reward." The name *Issachar* comes from the Hebrew word *yissakar*, which is the combination of two words: *nasa* meaning "to lift, advance, arise, bring forth, exalt, raise up" and *sakar* meaning "payment of contract, salary, fare, hire, price, reward, wages, worth." Leah was saying: "Issachar will bring a reward to me. He will make my pain and sacrifice worth it all."

The Issachar anointing will bring blessing and God's reward. He is faithful to reward those who diligently seek Him even through difficulty (see Hebrews 11:6). He will cause all the pain and struggle you have been through to produce God's purpose in your life. As you discern God's times and align with His plan, you will be able to say, "He has made my pain and sacrifice worth it all!"

Conceiving the Issachar Anointing

To walk in the Issachar anointing of prophetic discernment, leadership, alignment, intercession, prosperity and reward involves sacrifice. Just as Rachel paid a price with her heart and Leah paid a price to conceive this anointing, there is a price to be paid to walk in it. It is conceived by going through the travail of challenges, heartbreak and perseverance. This anointing from God turns our pain into promise, but as Leah declared, "Issachar will bring a reward that will make all my pain and sacrifice worth it."

Issachar was conceived during the wheat harvest, a season connected to the feast of Pentecost. In the New Testament God chose to give birth to His Church on the Day of Pentecost as the Holy Spirit was poured out. From that day forward the disciples went forth, oftentimes operating in the Issachar anointing of discernment, and turned the world upside down (see Acts 17:6).

Today we can receive fresh fire from heaven, just as the early Church did at Pentecost. As we encounter God and His supernatural power in a new way, and as He stirs up the spirit man within, we can, like the early disciples in Acts 2, birth the power to change nations.

Birthing Breakthrough

Issachar was the ninth son of Jacob. The number nine in Hebrew, *tet*, means "to sweep out by judgment, goodness and humility." This is the character of Issachar.

As a woman gives birth in the ninth month so will the Church begin to birth the breakthroughs we have been carrying, releasing a time of fruitfulness, blessing, joy, fulfillment and harvest. Scholars say *tet* is associated with the picture of a pregnant woman. A pregnant woman is said to be "expecting." I hear the challenge of the Holy Spirit as He asks us, *What are you expecting?* We must move past disappointments and fears from past seasons of barrenness or spiritual stillbirths and stir up a revival of our expectations before God to see our faith produce the breakthrough we have discerned and carried.

As a woman completes her ninth month her discomfort increases until the delivery. Sometimes she even feels miserable with emotions, sleepless nights and pressure . . . but there is a joy set before her. That joy will give grace to endure the times of challenge, knowing that when it becomes time to push, her life will change forever.

Those carrying the Issachar anointing understand spiritual labor pains and travail to birth. I have found that times of change and visitation are always preceded by times of intense burdens of prayer and seeking God. As you discern the times, you will know when it is time to push!

A Charge to Issachar

As we are entering the time of the Third Great Awakening in the earth, it becomes vital for every believer to operate in an Issachar anointing, to understand God's prophetic times and to know what to do in order to align with His divine purposes.

It is also time for Issachar-type leaders to arise. God is raising up a new breed of spiritual fathers and mothers who know how to birth His purposes in the earth by listening to His voice, discerning the times and pressing forward through intercession, expectation and declaration. These leaders will have a strong ability to understand God's times as well as have wisdom and strategy to advance and even prosper in the midst of shaking.

Arise, Issachar, for He will bring a reward!

ACTIVATION

What are you expecting from God? Now that you have studied the characteristics of the Issachar anointing, identify the traits you see operating in your life most prominently. Also identify the traits you feel God most wants to develop in you. Now, in a time of praying in the Spirit, allow God to birth something new in your life, expanding your ability to discern the times and know what to do.

4

HAVING A
DISCERNING HEART

"So give your servant a discerning heart to govern
your people and to distinguish between right and
wrong. For who is able to govern this great people
of yours?"

1 Kings 3:9 NIV

Discernment is an incredible gift that enables believers
to see into the realm of the spirit. This gift helps us to
distinguish between demonic spirits, angelic spirits and even
the human spirit. It aids in prayer, in deliverance, in leadership,
in business and in prophetic ministry. It strengthens the life of
every believer by showing us what is happening in our own
hearts and thought processes.

The gifts of the Holy Spirit are generally externalized to
bless and build the whole Body of Christ, yet the gifts can and
should have impact on the lives of those operating in them.

As a prophet, I lay my hands on others and release the word of the Lord, but I also have learned to listen to God's voice in my personal life for guidance and strategy. I operate in gifts of healings but when I personally need healing I can activate that same anointing from Christ to pray and believe for my own healing. As one who operates in discerning of spirits, I could find it easy merely to externalize the gift and see angels and demons in the spirit realm affecting others, yet never allow it to distinguish and judge issues going on in my own life. It is just as important for discernment to work in us and for us as it is for discernment to work through us!

House Cleaning

During the early years of our marriage Tom and I relocated several times. With each transition we boxed up new memories that went with us to each new home. When we moved into our current residence we decided to go through every box before it went up into the attic to be sure we knew what we were saving.

So in our new season we started cleaning out all the old boxes in storage. Wow! What a bunch of junk! There were whole boxes of worthless papers, old clothes that reminded us we were no longer that size and even several boxes of rocks. Yep! Rocks. These were part of a collection of boxes labeled "Tom's Treasures," which were things he had collected and stored during his childhood.

Some of the things in those boxes were scary. There was a raccoon tail that he had cut off a dead raccoon by the side of the road. It was disgusting. Along with that was an eagle's claw he had found that still had a tendon attached so that when you pulled it the claw opened and shut. These were the things Tom had cherished as a boy, and they had followed us from home to home sealed tightly in boxes.

Sadly, this is often how we live our spiritual lives. As we move from season to season we store up old junk: unforgiveness, fear, anxiety, hardness of heart, vain imaginations, hurt and even some demonic attachments. These become a part of the landscape of our lives, and we seal them up inside, just as "Tom's Treasures" were sealed. Discernment aids us in ripping the lids off the boxes and digging out, examining and discarding the things that rob us of our victory and freedom in Christ.

But the story does not end there.

We were ruthless in getting rid of the old junk. By the time we had gone through the boxes we had half a garage full of garbage. It was ready to be thrown out. But for some reason putting all that junk out on the street for the garbage collector to haul away was embarrassing to me.

I said to Tom, "Maybe we can put it out little by little so we don't look like such trashy people."

Tom just laughed and said we needed to put it all out. We needed to get the trash out of our house and be done with it.

That is how it is with deliverance sometimes. We want to get cleaned out and refreshed spiritually, but we would rather not have anyone see how much junk we have to get free from. Discerning our need for freedom, however, is not a shameful thing; it should be a part of our walk in the Holy Spirit as we pursue purity and holiness.

Discernment helps us see in the spirit what we cannot see with our natural eyes or understand with our natural minds. When Tom and I receive ministry from our deliverance team leaders, we encourage them to activate their spiritual discernment. If they sense that we have allowed something in our lives that resists or hinders the work of the Holy Spirit in us, or is harassing us or somehow affecting our souls, we gladly repent when repentance is called for and allow them to minister deliverance to us. The gift of discernment makes us stronger spiritually, emotionally and physically.

Solomon's Need

Solomon had a rocky start to being king.

King David's days on earth were fading, and he had yet to proclaim publicly which one of his sons was heir to the throne. His oldest son, Amnon, had already been murdered by son number three, Absalom, and later Absalom, who conspired to be king, was killed during his rebellion. David was aware of the tension between his remaining sons, yet God had made it clear who his successor was. David had subsequently promised Bathsheba that her son, Solomon, who was younger than David's sons mentioned here, would sit upon the throne.

In the meantime, son number four, Adonijah, was proclaiming himself to be king and throwing a big party complete with sacrifices and great feasting. David's former general named Joab, Abiathar the priest and all the king's other sons except Solomon were celebrating at this coronation party—when Nathan the prophet and Bathsheba brought the crisis to David's attention.

That very day David directed Nathan, Zadok the priest and Benaiah the warrior to take Solomon to Gihon to be anointed king. A crowd of people watched the anointing ceremony and heard the proclamation. As Solomon traveled back to Jerusalem to be seated on the throne, the people began to celebrate and shout, "Long live King Solomon!" Needless to say this put a damper on Adonijah's coronation party. He and his men had to humble themselves so as not to incur the wrath of their new king.

Solomon gave Joab and Abiathar second chances at life with stipulations of loyalty and obedience. And he showed mercy initially to Adonijah. After all, Adonijah was quite likely David's oldest surviving son and could have been expected to be David's natural successor.

Then one day Adonijah made a seemingly innocent request. He asked Solomon's mother, Bathsheba, for a favor. Would she use her influence with Solomon to gain him a consolation prize for not being king? All he wanted was permission to have a young woman named Abishag as his wife. What could possibly be wrong with that request?

The Abishag Trap

Abishag, a Shunammite, was a lovely young woman who was selected to attend to King David in his final years. She cared for the king, served him and warmed his bed though she remained a virgin. It was an honored position for a young woman of that time. So why did this request for her to become his wife precipitate Adonijah's execution? Solomon discerned the evil intent behind the request.

If you recall, when Absalom overthrew David and took control of the royal palace, the first thing he did was to take David's concubines up on the rooftop and have sexual relations with them in the view of the people. There was a cultural understanding that if you replaced the king in his bed, you were also replacing the king on his throne.

Thus, Adonijah's request had subversion written all over it. Solomon discerned it and had Adonijah, his older brother, executed.

Charles Spurgeon said, "Discernment isn't just knowing the difference between right and wrong. Often it is knowing between right and almost right." Solomon was able to discern the motive behind Adonijah's request. I have heard that rat poison is 99 percent good food and 1 percent poison, but it is enough to kill the rat.

Solomon also had Joab executed, for Joab was in this conspiracy with Adonijah. Joab had served as David's general but had allowed bitterness to cloud his heart. He was the one who had killed Absalom during his rebellion, defying David's specific order, out of a sense of vengeance and false justice. This and other like events caused him to become out of alignment with the throne, and he switched his loyalties to Adonijah. Had he properly discerned his own heart, his life may have been saved.

Solomon had the priest Abiathar deposed and banished to his home, considering him to be part of the conspiracy as well. These men had served David faithfully, but they failed to discern their own hearts, God's choice for king and the new season in Israel, leading them to rebel and setting themselves up for judgment.

Malachi 3:18 says, "Then you shall again discern between the righteous and the wicked, between one who serves God and one who does not serve him." The decisions regarding these men were not the result of Solomon's ambition or suspicion; rather, they served as instances in which Solomon needed to judge his own heart and then properly discern the hearts of others.

Solomon's Dream

As you might imagine, these early days of Solomon's reign could have shaken his confidence. Perhaps he began to feel overwhelmed by his inadequacies. After all, he was the son of Bathsheba, the woman his father had committed adultery with and whose husband he had murdered to cover his sin. He was neither the oldest son in line for the throne nor a great warrior. Several who had faithfully served his father failed to give their loyalty to him; in return he had ordered their executions or banishment. He could have thought, *Am I really called to be king?* He recognized he was going to need God's supernatural help if he was going to fulfill his calling and rule the nation well.

We read that Solomon went up to Gibeon and offered one thousand burnt offerings, crying out to God for help. God met him in a dream and imparted a supernatural gift of discernment, understanding and wisdom. He awoke as the wisest man to ever live!

> "Now, LORD my God, you have made your servant king in place of my father David. But I am only a little child and do not know how to carry out my duties. Your servant is here among the people you have chosen, a great people, too numerous to count or number. So give your servant a discerning heart to govern your people and to distinguish between right and wrong. For who is able to govern this great people of yours?"
>
> The LORD was pleased that Solomon had asked for this. So God said to him, "Since you have asked for this and not for long life or wealth for yourself, nor have asked for the death of your enemies but for discernment in administering justice, I will do what you have asked. I will give you a wise and discerning heart, so that there will never have been anyone like you, nor will there ever be. Moreover, I will give you what you have not asked for—both wealth and honor—so that in your lifetime you will have no equal among kings. And if you walk in obedience to me and keep my decrees and commands as David your father did, I will give you a long life." Then Solomon awoke—and he realized it had been a dream.
>
> 1 Kings 3:7–15 NIV

A Leader's Prayer

Solomon cried out to God in his dream that he was only a child and did not know how to carry out his duties. He had some pretty big shoes to fill, and in light of all the trouble, he was overwhelmed by the responsibility of leading such a great nation. So he asked for a discerning heart so he could govern well.

This should be the humble prayer of every leader.

The word translated "discerning heart" in Hebrew is *shama*, which, as I mentioned earlier, means "to listen intentionally and to hear intelligently." It also means "to pay attention, to be certain, to discern, to understand, to listen and yield to." Solomon was saying, "Lord, I need the ability to lead through listening to Your voice and yielding to Your wisdom, which is above my own. As I hear Your voice I will be able to discern things properly and be empowered to fulfill my leadership calling with wisdom, certainty and intelligence. I am not on my own; Your voice will empower me to be a good leader."

Solomon's request pleased the Lord. Because having clear discernment to lead was Solomon's priority and the thing his heart desired above riches, long life or power over his enemies, God granted his request and made him the wisest, most discerning man who ever lived. Having the ability to discern his own heart, the hearts of others and the destiny of his nation was a gift from God. God told him He would give him what he asked for—a discerning heart—plus give him what he did not ask for—riches and honor and fame. His pursuit of a discerning heart led to good success and caused every blessing to come to his life.

Once Solomon discerned his own heart properly, he was able to discern the hearts of others. We see evidence of this in the next part of Solomon's story when two women came to him arguing over a baby. God showed him a strategy to determine the identity of the baby's mother, a strategy that allowed him to discern what was in their hearts.

Discerning Our Own Hearts

Hebrews 4:12 says, "The word of God is living and powerful, and sharper than any two-edged sword, piercing even to the division of soul and spirit, and of joints and marrow, and is a discerner of the thoughts and intents of the heart." Part of the gift of discerning of spirits is to discern what may be occurring in the human heart. Clearly before we can discern what is taking place in the hearts of others, we must tend to our own hearts.

Solomon wrote about the condition of the heart and warned us to keep it in alignment with God: "Keep your heart with all diligence for out of it flow the issues of life" (Proverbs 4:23), and "He that trusts in his own heart is a fool" (Proverbs 28:26).

Our human hearts, if left unchecked, can and will lead us astray. Discernment can be the antidote for invading, toxic thoughts and emotions that cloud our spiritual perception. It uncovers impure, pride-filled or selfish heart motivations that sabotage our walk with God. Discernment enables us to pursue the presence of God with clean hands, a pure heart and a clear conscience and experience the glory of God in a tangible way.

Our Hearts Need Guarding

The apostle Paul also challenges us regarding the condition of our hearts: "Be anxious for nothing, but in everything by prayer and supplication, with thanksgiving, let your requests be made known to God; and the peace of God, which surpasses all understanding, will guard your hearts and minds through Christ Jesus" (Philippians 4:6–7). The Greek word translated "guard" is *phroureo*. It is a military term that means "to be a watcher in advance, to place a protective military guard or sentinel at the gate to prevent hostile invasion, to keep and protect for the purpose of attaining something in the future." The word *hearts* refers to emotions, affections, passions, desires and feelings, and the word *minds* refers to thoughts, intellect, reasoning and perceptions.

Wow! The peace of God will act as a military sentinel at the gates of our hearts and minds to guard against hostile invading thoughts, feelings, emotions or reasoning in order to protect and preserve our futures.

I once dreamed that I was driving down the road when I saw something on the side of the road that I needed to attend to. I pulled my car over and jumped out, leaving the door open, and rushed to tend to matters. When I returned I jumped into the car, shut the door and tried to start the engine, but my battery was dead. I tried over and over to get the engine to start to no avail.

When I woke up from the dream I began to pray about it. I had been very busy traveling to numerous nations plus handling the responsibilities of church and family at home. I was exhausted. So when I began to pray about the dead battery in the dream I thought it had to do with the business of my schedule and being worn down.

But as I prayed I heard the Lord say to me, *The dream isn't about the dead battery but about the open door that caused it!* The open door represented access points that I had left unguarded in my soul that were causing me to be worn out, whether from demonic attack or simply just neglect. Discernment helped me close the door and get my battery charged to go again!

Discernment—a Gift and a Choice

Solomon became an amazing king, a tremendous builder and a poet. He wrote more than three thousand proverbs and more than one thousand songs. He built the Temple in Jerusalem and the wall around the city as well as a palace that was envied by royalty from afar. He was wealthy beyond imagination. Where his father, David, had been a valiant warrior, Solomon was a brilliant military strategist with a strong infantry, cavalry and navy. He taught botany and animal sciences. He developed successful trade routes, and the nation prospered under his rule.

He was known as the wisest man who ever lived; however, he ended up living a life of sin, idolatry and greed. He famously had three hundred wives and seven hundred concubines, and according to 1 Kings 11:4 these wives "turned his heart after other gods." Yes, he built a magnificent Temple for Yahweh, the one true God, but he also built temples for the goddess Ashtoreth, the abominable Milcom (or Molech) and other gods and goddesses. At the end of his life he was disillusioned and proclaimed every venture to be but "vanity" (Ecclesiastes 1:14).

How could this happen to the wisest, most discerning man who ever lived? We must realize that discernment is both a gift and a choice. Once we discern the leading of the Lord we must obey. What good does it do to discern and not obey? What good is it to have clear, prophetic insight, wisdom and knowledge if we are going to choose to live after the desires of our flesh? I have been in ministry long enough to know that being discerning or prophetically gifted does not inoculate one against sin; rather, it gives the opportunity to see the hostile invasion of demonic or human thought and reject it before it takes its toll. Exercising a gift is one thing. Exercising the choice to live holy lives is another.

Solomon became vulnerable to sin during the most prosperous time in his life. If we are not careful that can become a template that leads to our downfalls as well. When we are pressing in and battling, struggling to discern and then establish the plans of God in our lives, we are usually diligent to guard our hearts to stay in strong relationship and be pleasing to God.

But what about times of abundant blessing? Are we equally as diligent, passionate and purposeful in our times of blessing as we are in times of difficulty? We must stay sharp and not let down our guard, realizing that the enemy of our souls will look for an opportunity to take us captive or lead us astray. We are especially vulnerable after a great victory. We must maintain diligence before, during and after the battle and give no place to the devil (see Ephesians 4:27).

At times in his life Solomon was able to express great words of wisdom, realizing not only his successes but also his failures. Here is what he had to say about wisdom and discernment:

My child, will you treasure my wisdom? Then, and only then, will you acquire it. And only if you accept my advice and hide it within will you succeed. So train your heart to listen when I speak and open your spirit wide to expand your discernment—then pass it on to your sons and daughters. . . . For if you keep seeking it like a man would seek for sterling silver, searching in hidden places for cherished treasure, then you will discover the fear of the Lord and find the true knowledge of God. Wisdom is a gift from a generous God, and every word he speaks is full of revelation and becomes a fountain of understanding within you. For the Lord has a hidden storehouse of wisdom made accessible to his godly lovers. He becomes your personal bodyguard as you follow his ways, protecting and guarding you as you choose what is right. Then you will discover all that is just, proper, and fair, and be empowered to make the right decisions as you walk into your destiny. When wisdom wins your heart and revelation breaks in, true pleasure enters your soul. If you choose to follow good counsel, divine design will watch over you and understanding will protect you from making poor choices. It will rescue you from evil in disguise and from those who speak duplicities.

Proverbs 2:1–2, 4–12 TPT

ACTIVATION

Invite the peace of God to guard your heart and mind, to guard against hostile invading thoughts, feelings, emotions or reasoning in order to protect and preserve your future. Say yes to the Lord for this wonderful gift of discernment and make a fresh commitment to choose to live in obedience to His will and in His ways.

5

DISCERNMENT TO LEAD

"Here's what I want: Give me a God-listening heart
so I can lead your people well, discerning the difference between good and evil. For who on their own
is capable of leading your glorious people?"

1 Kings 3:9 MESSAGE

In his book *Developing the Leader Within You* (Nelson, 1993),
John Maxwell defines *leadership* as "influence." Every be-
liever should desire to lead in some way to extend and expand
God's Kingdom.

I love being a leader! I love having the opportunity to pour
God's heart into lives and see people become everything God
has created them to be. I love the influence God gives leaders
to help individuals fulfill their destinies and find their callings.
But I do not necessarily love confrontation or dealing with hard
issues or situations of discipline in people's lives. I have prayed
Solomon's prayer many times—asking that I have a wise and
discerning heart so that I can be an effective leader. I cannot

imagine trying to be in a place of spiritual responsibility without the gift of discernment.

As I was growing as a discerning leader I had many experiences when what I discerned in the spirit showed no evidence in the natural. One woman came into our church with a quiet demeanor and a peaceful expression on her face. But when I looked at her I saw a swirl of demonic powers over her head, and I knew she was fearful and tormented. When I took her aside and shared with her what I saw, she burst into tears and asked if she could speak privately with Tom and me. She told us that she was in hiding from an abusive ex-husband who was involved in Satanism. Through years of physical and emotional abuse she had mastered the art of presenting a peaceful facade even though her inner world was in turmoil. The gift of discernment brought her out from behind her walls so that she could get help.

On another occasion I knew a young man who had been accused of a crime. He seemed to have such a sweet heart; it honestly seemed impossible to me that he could be guilty of the crime he was accused of. When Tom and I asked him about it, he told us that he was innocent. But that night I had a dream. I was in a room when a poisonous snake came out of the closet. I hate snakes so I ran to get my husband to deal with it. When I came back into the room the snake was gone. In its place was a cute, fluffy puppy. But when I picked up the puppy I saw that it had the eyes of the snake. I knew then that what seemed to be innocent was actually something else entirely. Discernment enabled us to deal properly with this individual as he faced the charges and was convicted for the crime he had committed.

Discerning Spiritual Authority

Solomon had a heart to govern or rule God's people well. His father was a great king and was loved by God and the people.

He was not a perfect man, but he exemplified having a perfect heart toward God, even in his failures. David was a good ruler, and now Solomon was sitting on his throne.

Part of being a good leader is to have proper understanding of holding positions of spiritual authority while also being *under* spiritual authority; we need careful discernment regarding those in leadership over us. If our discernment of our leaders considers only the flesh, we will fail to position ourselves properly when things get challenging. I believe that it was Adonijah's failure to discern his proper relationship to the appointed authority, his father the king, that resulted in the throne being passed to his brother.

Solomon did not grasp after the throne but waited until his father authorized his coronation. He had watched his brothers Absalom and Adonijah fail to discern true authority. Part of his success at being in authority was that he had learned first to be a man under authority.

He also had the example of his father who, though he had been anointed king by the prophet Samuel, discerned the situation and continued to honor Saul as his appointed leader. The truth is, God's hand had lifted from Saul but he was still in position as the rightful king over Israel. He despised David because the hand of the Lord was upon him, and he sought to kill him.

But David continued to keep his heart right and refused to touch God's anointed, or even God's once-anointed, even when it might have seemed as though God had delivered Saul into his hand. Saul was crazy, but he was still king. David discerned the proper order of authority and fought for Israel against their enemies even while Saul plotted his death.

David had such a sense of honor toward Saul that when news came of Saul's death on the battlefield, David wept and his men wept (see 2 Samuel 1:11–12). Though Saul did it all wrong and tried to kill David for years, David kept a proper perspective about authority, which instilled honor in his men as well. Rather than celebrate the death of their mortal enemy, they mourned the death of their king.

Gene Edwards, author of *A Tale of Three Kings* (Tyndale, 1992), wrote this: "King Saul sought to destroy David, but his only success was that he became the instrument of God to put to death the Saul who roamed about in the caverns of David's own soul." In other words, God put David under Saul to kill the Saul in David. We must properly discern our relationships with our spiritual leaders or we will find ourselves grasping after something that should instead be given. Absalom grasped after a crown. Adonijah grasped after a throne. Solomon waited for the kingdom to be passed to him.

As leaders, we must remember that the enemy's plan is always to feed human ambition and pride in order to separate us from our true spiritual leaders. He will create misunderstanding and controversy and encourage pride in an attempt to destroy relationships or disrupt generational continuity and legacy. Gene Edwards also said: "The Sauls of this world can never see a David; they only see Absalom. The Absaloms of this world can never see a David; they see only Saul."

Discerning the Why Behind the What

As leaders, recognizing that we are both under authority and at the same time in authority over others, it is very important that we are able to look past external actions to see the brokenness of a person's heart or life, which may precipitate immature or unhealthy behaviors. We need to recognize that a person may be yelling on the outside but crying on the inside. We must walk in discernment, looking past the obvious things in the natural to see the root of pain and dysfunction in the soul. Hurting people hurt people, but as we properly discern the root, we will be better equipped to bind up the broken heart and heal the wounded soul.

A dear friend of mine, Nancy Alcorn, is founder and president of Mercy Multiplied, formerly Mercy Ministries, a transformation ministry for young women. Young ladies come in with life-controlling issues such as drugs, alcohol, human trafficking, sexual abuse, unplanned pregnancies, self-harm, etc., and leave transformed and empowered by the word and presence of God in their lives.

When Nancy was starting her career, she worked for the state of Tennessee in the correctional facility for delinquent girls. She often saw young women making bad choices in their lives, establishing patterns that took them in and out of the corrections system, sometimes for life. These young women were hardened by life at an early age.

Later Nancy worked in emergency child protective services and saw some of the most horrific abuse, neglect and trauma that a child could possibly suffer. God spoke to Nancy, overlaying the image of a particular woman in the corrections system with the scene of an abused child, and said, *I am showing you the "why" behind the "what."*

When we know the "why" behind the "what," we must allow this to motivate us with Christ's love and mercy. Nancy challenges us: "We must have compassion for people we don't understand. We have not walked where they have walked . . . when judgment is present, compassion is absent."

In her book *Echoes of Mercy* (Mercy Ministries, 2008), Nancy shares the revelation that led to the birth of her ministry, which has brought transformation to the lives of thousands of young women:

> The state cannot bring restoration to broken lives—it is unequipped for the task. The reason is simple: God has not anointed the government to "bind up the broken hearted" or to "proclaim liberty to the captives." He has anointed the church. We are to set them free.

All of us have a "why" behind our "what," things in our lives that have set us up to make bad decisions and wrong choices. Good leaders will see that our ultimate responsibility is to set captives free. To do that we must ask God to show us the "why" behind the "what" in the lives of those we are called to minister to.

Setting Captives Free

Here is an example. Some time ago a woman attended our church who seemed fervent in worship and intercession. She was growing in her spiritual walk. But there was something about her that I discerned was not right. I did not want to be guilty of being judgmental, so I prayed that God would show me what the problem was.

Then I noticed something. She loved to lay hands on people and pray for them. Her heart's desire seemed to be to bless others. But soon I began to notice that after she prayed for people, bad things happened to them. She laid hands on one young man, and he fell off a ladder and broke his shoulder a few hours later. One woman was hit by a car while crossing the street just a day after this woman prayed for her. Yet another person became deathly ill within a few days of this woman's prayers. Coincidence? Maybe, but I felt it warranted further exploration, so Tom and I asked her to come and talk with us.

I mentioned what I had noticed, trying hard not to bring any accusation against her since she seemed genuinely to want to serve and please the Lord. She began to cry and said that this kind of thing always happened to her.

We began to ask her about her life in order to discern the "why" behind the "what" so we could bring her into freedom. It turns out her mother was a witch who dedicated her to Satan at an early age. She also lived in a relationship with a warlock until she gave her life to Jesus. Since being saved, she had never received the ministry of deliverance from the demonic attachments in her life, so we suggested doing that.

Tom and I fasted several days and then met with her to begin the ministry of deliverance. Her face contorted as different demonic spirits came out of her. The difference in her was dramatic. Her entire countenance changed right before our eyes. She looked so free! She came to the service that night and practically glowed with the presence of the Lord as she worshiped.

But two days later she came to church, and I saw all the demonic things back on her. Her face no longer glowed with peace; now she looked troubled and tormented. What had changed?

We met with her again to ask what happened.

"I don't know," she answered. "I spent several hours in intercession yesterday and ever since then I have felt the same oppression over my life."

Suddenly, I discerned that her intercession was the issue, which seemed like a strange thing to me.

"Please describe for me what happens when you intercede," I said. I knew there was something not right here.

She explained, "When I pray, my spirit leaves my body and meets up with my prayer angel, who has been with me my whole life. My prayer angel tells me how to pray."

I knew what was happening. This was not an angel, but a spirit guide, a demonic guardian spirit who was assigned over her life when her mother dedicated her to Satan. It was masquerading as an angel when in fact it was a demonic spirit attached to her. Because of this, whenever she laid hands on people there was transference of the spirit of witchcraft, which caused accidents, calamity and sickness.

It took her a while to be willing to cut off access to this spirit because it had been with her since her infancy and masqueraded as her friend. But eventually she repented, and we cast this spirit out of her. She was truly set free. She was then able to become the intercessor God had originally created her to be.

Discerning God's Process

When the devil is causing someone trouble, we have the authority and power to bind him and cast him out. But how do you handle the situation when the trouble is part of God's own process to conform the individual to the image of Christ?

You might feel a certain objection at first to the suggestion that God would trouble a person. Remember, however, God has never been afraid to test and try the righteous. As leaders we must discern whether the trouble is an attack from the enemy or a test from God to shape the individual's character, making him or her ready for a time of promotion in the call and destiny of God. Bishop Hamon has always said that God will make the man before the mighty ministry. Put another way, God will prepare the person before the position.

Joseph, for example, had prophetic dreams of a great calling. Then all hell broke loose in his life: He was betrayed by his brothers, sold into slavery, falsely accused, thrown into prison. You could make a case that the devil was tormenting and harassing him because of his calling. Yet, it was this process that prepared him for his destiny to rule a nation. Scripture makes this clear: "The word of the LORD tried him" (Psalm 105:19 KJV). During this process God transformed him from a shepherd to a man who understood agriculture, government and leadership, which made him ready for his time of rulership.

Abraham was asked to sacrifice his son Isaac. Abraham could have rebuked the devil and moved on, but it was a test from God that shaped his character. Scripture actually says this: "God tested Abraham" (Genesis 22:1). When Abraham made preparation for the sacrifice God stopped him and said,

> "Now I know that you fear God. . . . Because you have done this thing, and have not withheld your son, your only son— blessing I will bless you, and multiplying I will multiply your

descendants . . . and your descendants shall possess the gate of their enemies."

Genesis 22:12, 16–17

Abraham discerned the voice of God and cooperated with God's testing process.

It is crucial for leaders to discern whether to bind the devil and do deliverance or to lead the person in a prayer of repentance from wrong thoughts and attitudes or to encourage the person forward who is experiencing God's testing process— which we dare not pray them out of. We cannot protect people from God's maturing process. In this situation we pray for grace, wisdom and peace in their souls and a speedy ability to learn whatever lessons God is teaching.

Discernment in Business

A businessman in our church came to us in a desperate situation. He had always been successful in his business dealings and had no problem making money. He seemed to have a golden touch on everything he put his hand to—until he became a Christian. Since he gave his heart to the Lord, he struggled to prosper even though it seemed it should be the other way around. He paid his tithes and was a generous giver; however, his recent real estate deals were going badly, and he was facing bankruptcy if something did not change. We prayed with him and asked the Lord for discernment about what was happening.

That night Tom had a dream where he saw the businessman, a spiritual medium and a deck of cards. Suddenly, the cards came alive and began flying around the room chasing the man. Tom woke up and knew there was a key in this dream that would set the man free to prosper.

The next day we met with him again. Tom shared his dream and asked if the man ever had any dealings with a medium or fortune-teller. He initially said no, but then he thought again. Yes, as a young man he went into a tent at a fair and spoke with a medium. She asked him for a dollar bill. When he handed it to her, she folded it in a specific way and chanted some kind of spell over the dollar and handed it back to him. She told him that as long as he kept this in his wallet he would prosper and succeed.

He pulled out his wallet and removed that folded dollar bill, which he had carried with him all those years. There was a curse attached. As long as he served the devil, he prospered, but as soon as he began to serve the Lord, the devil cut off his prosperity. The man repented and we broke the curse. Within days he had several contracts on different pieces of real estate. Discernment removed the blockages and released the ability to prosper.

Solomon was an extremely wealthy king and an astute businessman. He dealt with King Hiram of Tyre, and had favor with other kings in the surrounding areas. He developed trade routes and through them turned enemies into allies. This was part of the blessing that came to Solomon when he requested the gift and ability of discernment in leadership over the nation. God will give discernment in business dealings, in hiring people, in showing you whom to deal with and how to prosper.

When we were praying about moving the ministry of Christian International from Phoenix, Arizona, Bishop and Mom Hamon learned of a ministry partnership opportunity with a man who was developing land in the panhandle of Florida. We all knew we were supposed to move to that general area, and in the natural it seemed like a perfect fit. He was a Christian and had a similar vision as the one God had given to Bishop Hamon. The land was beautiful and inexpensive and was going to be dedicated to building a ministry base. It all seemed perfect— except for one thing: Mom Hamon and I did not have a good feeling about it. When everything seems perfect and your gut says something is wrong, there is a reason.

Mom Hamon and I expressed our concerns about how we felt but really could not point to any specific reason for feeling as we did. Remember, at the time there was not much teaching about discernment, and everything seemed perfect, so we went ahead with the deal and bought land with him.

Well, it was not long before we all discovered that the man had been dishonest with us. When we confronted him, we ended up in a very hostile situation. By the grace of God we were able to get out of the partnership, but had we paid attention to the discernment we would have saved ourselves a great deal of trouble.

Discernment to Govern

The anointing of wisdom and discernment given by God to Solomon not only made him a great leader of his people but also gave him favor and influence with other leaders. He was sought after for his wisdom by other kings, queens and national leaders:

> All the kings of Arabia and the governors of the land brought gold and silver to Solomon. . . . King Solomon was greater in riches and wisdom than all the other kings of the earth. All the kings of the earth sought audience with Solomon to hear the wisdom God had put in his heart.
>
> 2 Chronicles 9:14, 22–23 NIV1984

Solomon did business with the queen of Sheba, the kings of Arabia and the governors of the land.

God wants to give wise, discerning, prophetic leaders favor with civic leaders, corporate leaders and even national leaders so they, too, can hear the wisdom of God and the word of the Lord to help them advance.

The Old Testament prophets often spoke the word of the Lord to kings and often discerned the things that would cause the kings and their nations to be out of alignment with God's plan and blessings. The same is true in modern days. God will raise up those like Jeremiah who have this anointing and calling: "See, I have this day set you over the nations and over the kingdoms, to root out and to pull down, to destroy and to throw down, to build and to plant" (Jeremiah 1:10).

While Tom and I, and many other prophetic ministers, have spoken to national leaders in different parts of the world, one of the most remarkable stories of national transformation began in 1993 in the Philippines. That year Bishop Hamon prophesied to then president-elect Fidel Ramos. He was the first Protestant president elected in an otherwise half-Catholic, half-Muslim nation. The word of the Lord to him was that God was going to use him to begin a transformation process in the land that would expose corruption in the government, bring revival to the church and cause the Philippines to be transformed from a Third World nation to a First World economy. On hearing these words, the prophetic church began to wage war in prayer to see this word for the nation fulfilled. The prophecy was published in the newspapers, shown on television and played on the radio, so the whole land heard it and had the opportunity to come into agreement with the word of the Lord.

Over the next several years God began to uproot the corruption entrenched in the government and began a whole new era in the nation, which caused foreign investors to view it as a more stable economy. Today the economy of the Philippines is thriving, the government is stable, and, best of all, the Church has experienced an incredible revival with millions of born-again Christians attending services each Sunday. Now there are Christians serving in government as senators, governors, mayors, judges and other roles, many of whom have received prophetic words about their personal destinies and callings to their nation. It is a nation in transformation that was initiated by a prophetic word that discerned the nation's true identity in the earth.

Discerning Leaders Arise!

Just as Solomon was led by supernatural wisdom, discernment and revelation, so, too, God is looking for leaders to arise in cultural pursuits, in business, in media, in education, in government—all to bring a Kingdom perspective and influence. These men and women will have to deal with human ambition and must instead be motivated by a holy, passionate pursuit of God's Kingdom and His people. God is opening the heavens and releasing clear, prophetic perspectives and anointed discernment upon His leaders in order to increase favor and influence until the "kingdoms of this world have become the kingdoms of our Lord and of His Christ" (Revelation 11:15).

ACTIVATION

Pray and ask the Lord to show you how you are called to be a leader. Consider how God has positioned you, both in authority as well as under authority. Have there been times under another's leadership that were particularly challenging for you because you had to deal with "Saul" type character traits in your own heart or life? What do you discern was God's process of character development for you? What are some specific areas of freedom and maturity He has brought into your life because of it?

6

DISCERNMENT TO BUILD

"I will build my church, and the gates of hell shall not prevail against it."

Matthew 16:18 ESV

One of the congregations within the network of our ministry had just purchased a building for its church family to use, and Tom and I were invited to participate in a dedication service. There was a great deal of excitement during the time of worship, for they were launching into a new season of being established in the community.

As I worshiped, I saw a vision of the foundation of the building. It had cracks and fractures running through it. As I watched, things began to shake, and the building began to crumble.

This hardly seemed to be an uplifting, celebratory type of word to share on this day of dedication, but I knew that God was showing me something important for their future. As I asked the Lord about it, He told me that what I was seeing was not about the physical structure of the building having literal cracks, nor was it about the spiritual foundation of the body of believers taking up residence there. God was showing me that previous congregations who had used this same building had been affected by a residing spirit of division. It had caused their congregations to crumble during times of shaking because their foundations were not stable and strong. I sensed that a religious spirit was actually rejoicing that a new church was moving in, because it had been so effective in destroying the last few congregations.

I shared this vision with the pastor, and he confirmed what the Lord had spoken to me. Several previous congregations had experienced division while in the building, and a religious spirit had kept them fighting over minor issues until they split or even closed down altogether.

This was a church in need of repair. It needed to be restored to the original idea of a gathering place for a congregation to worship God in unity in the city. We prayed and repented that day, at the time of dedication, and uprooted every assignment of the religious spirit and the spirit of division. We rebuked every territorial spirit that had laid claim to that property and evicted them in the spirit. We prayed that during this time of transition there would be a new beginning forged with unity, humility and influence for the Kingdom of God. Though every previous congregation ended its time in that facility with division, this church has now been there more than twenty years without ever experiencing a split. It has grown to be a voice of influence in the community, and God has blessed the people as they possess their land.

By comparison, there was another church that also had some things discerned that could have helped it move forward into a new season of successful building in their city. This church was in the Netherlands and had been a large Pentecostal church decades before. Tom and I had never been to this church, but we were scheduled to minister there.

Before leaving the United States I had a dream about it—that it was being attacked by one of the "ite" tribes of Canaan: the Perizzites (see Deuteronomy 7:1–7). The root word of the Hebrew word *perizzite* means "separation." I knew if they defeated this demonic force they would come into a time of growth, miracles and breakthrough. But if they did not rise up and fight back, this spiritual opposition would beat them.

As we arrived at the church for ministry, I saw and felt a black wave of darkness so strong it almost knocked me off my feet. We prayed and bound the spirit and went into the service. Tom preached about moving forward into their new season, then asked me to come up and share my dream. The pastor and many of the people began jumping to their feet and shouting in agreement with all we shared. They engaged fully with the word the Lord had given and cried out in repentance and engaged in spiritual warfare.

It seemed like breakthrough except for one thing. Sitting across the front row were the elders. They had their arms crossed and a frown of anger on their faces as if to say, "I shall not be moved." These were the ones who actually controlled the church. Within weeks after this service they fired the pastor. They believed he had spoken to us ahead of time about the tension between them and had then arranged for us to come and preach what we did.

Sadly, their story did not end the way we had hoped.

But there was still a happy ending . . . just not for that church. The fired pastor went to another city and many of the people followed him. He built a new church that was hungry for the move of God and desiring to see revival in the land. His church exploded in size, and the new city was touched by the power and presence of God.

Within the year the doors of his previous church were closed forever because of financial mismanagement and sin in the leadership. They failed to discern the attack of the enemy, the voice of God or His call to a new season.

This tale of two churches shows us that God is not just addressing the structures of various churches in various cities; He wants to restore the foundations of His global Church so we can be what we were originally created to be: the *ekklesia*—God's spiritual legislative body of rulers in the earth. There is a reformation underway, and we must have spiritual eyes and ears to discern it.

Religious Resistance to God's New Thing

Transition can be a tricky and vulnerable time. When things are changing it is more vital than ever to operate in discernment. As God begins to speak about "new seasons" and "new eras," we need to understand how to build in the new without despising the old; otherwise, we will miss the blessing of generational continuity.

We must be able to identify the workings of a religious spirit, which always resists change. It was the religious spirit that ultimately killed Christ and attempted to halt God's new move of reformation in the earth. The religious spirit tries constantly to create a form or structure with no power and will resist outpourings, revivals and restorations of truth, hoping to hold people in their past experiences. It will kill passionate prayer, joy and hunger for God and will bring weariness to the pioneers of change. The religious spirit will look for ways to create false comfort through rituals, methods and programs that diminish the active role of the voice of God and the demonstrated power of the Holy Spirit.

In the Kingdom of God, it really never is "Out with the old and in with the new" but rather "How do we appropriately connect the new to the previous order?" God is doing a new thing—but He is building it on what has been established in previous times. Just because God may be doing a new thing in apostolic or prophetic circles, does not mean we abandon the foundations laid about being justified by faith, baptism in water, holiness, healing, baptism with the Holy Spirit or any of the other previous restoration emphases of God's Spirit.

As a matter of fact, each of these moves failed to discern the new thing. Yes, Catholics persecuted Lutherans in the Protestant Reformation, but then Lutherans persecuted Baptists. Baptists persecuted Methodists. Methodists persecuted Pentecostals. Each move of restoration truth was persecuted by the previous move because the people failed to discern God's building process. They also failed to discern the religious spirit that was resisting forward advancement into a fresh revelation of God through His Word.

Solomon's Discernment in Building

Solomon recognized the challenge of transition, which precipitated his trip to the mountain to offer sacrifices and make a request for discernment. As we have seen, many who had faithfully followed David did not successfully navigate the transition into the new season. These men, Adonijah, Joab, Abiathar and others, recognized that a new season was coming, but they became presumptuous in defining what that new season would look like.

We have seen people do the same. God speaks indicating a new season, yet some, usually out of pride or ambition, jump in and label the past as an unnecessary "old order" and sever ties, rather than wisely building on the previously laid foundation of truth. Some, on the other hand, resist the "new thing" and try to hold on to the old, saying, "This isn't the way we did it before," rather than recognizing that change is often uncomfortable but necessary to fulfill God's call in the new day.

Solomon did neither. He recognized that his time upon the throne would look different from David's, but he did not try to break up the foundation laid by David. Nor did he try to live in the past to the detriment of moving forward; he discerned the new season with a new emphasis. David was a warrior king who spent time fighting enemies and establishing Israel as a kingdom in the earth. He discerned the times, knowing it was a time for war. Solomon also discerned the times, moving from a time of battling to a time of building. Yes, Solomon did go to war; he subdued the remaining enemies in the land. His reign, however, was more defined by what he built. He did not do the same things in the same way David did. He had a mandate, from a prophetic word given through David, to build a Temple for the living God. He built the Temple and his own palace and ushered in a time of great wealth and prestige for the kingdom of Israel.

Solomon's name comes from the root word *shalom* and means "to be safe, well, happy, healthy, prosperous, peaceful, to be completed, to be finished." He had an anointing to build and finish many things initiated by David. David's foundation was one of prophet, warrior and worshiper. Solomon navigated transition and built on all David had established and accomplished "according to the order of David, his father":

> And, according to the order of David his father, he appointed the divisions of the priests for their service, the Levites for their duties (to praise and serve before the priests) as the duty of each day required, and the gatekeepers by their divisions at each gate; for so David the man of God had commanded.
>
> 2 Chronicles 8:14

David prophesied regarding the house of God—he made plans and provision for it. Solomon appropriated all the provision and brought fulfillment to the plan. David established the Tabernacle with worship going up before the throne of God 24/7. He positioned the priests, worshipers and gatekeepers. Solomon maintained that same order and foundation, but he also ushered in the manifest glory of God's presence in the Temple; the priests could not even stand to minister because the glory of God was so thick. David prophesied and was a psalmist. Solomon had dreams from the Lord and also wrote songs and proverbs. David was a type of the prophetic, declaring what was to come. Solomon was a type of the apostolic, building and finishing with wisdom and strategy. David prepared the way for the future. Solomon honored the previous generation. David was a man of breakthrough. Solomon took it up another level and finished it!

"I Will Build My Church"

One day Jesus was walking and talking with His disciples when He asked them a question: "Who do men say that I am?"

His disciples had different answers: "Some say John the Baptist, some Elijah, and others Jeremiah or one of the prophets."

Then Jesus asked the big question: "But who do you say that I am?"

Simon Peter replied, "You are the Christ, the Son of the living God." He properly discerned who Jesus was as He walked among them.

Jesus went on to explain that this revelation did not come to Simon by natural means, by flesh and blood, but that he had been given revelation by the Father to see past the natural into the supernatural.

Now that His disciples understood who He was, they needed to know why He was on the earth. "I will build My church," He said, "and the gates of hell shall not prevail against it."

Jesus went on to shed His blood, die on the cross and be resurrected from the grave. This ushered in a whole new era in the earth. He was building His Church and laying the foundation with His own blood. It was a reformation! God was changing the rules of how man would relate to Him and find forgiveness for sin. Before this time a person had to bring an animal sacrifice to have his sin covered. Now the spotless Lamb of God had died as a sacrifice for the sin of mankind, for those who would believe on His name. No longer was sin covered; it was completely removed by the blood of Jesus. Everything changed.

Jesus is still building His Church today, and the gates of hell cannot prevail against it! The word *build* is the Greek word *oikodomeo* and means "to be a house-builder, to construct, to build from the foundation up, to restore by building, to repair, to establish, to edify." This is a reformation word. The word *prevail* is the Greek word *katischyo*, meaning "to overpower, to prevail, to be superior in strength, to overcome, to be strong against to another's detriment." This Church would be so amazingly powerful that the very gates of hell would not be able to overcome it! This was demonstrated by the early Church as they brought great transformation into cities and regions with signs, wonders and miracles occurring as the message of the Gospel of the Kingdom was preached. This period established Christianity in the earth. The reformation was in full progress.

Discernment in Reformation

But sadly, throughout the history of Christianity, we see a picture of a Church that, rather than overcoming, has often been overcome. Over time the Church failed to discern God's move or the working of the religious spirit of resistance and ended up becoming more of a political organization, having a form but no power. This was very evident when it fell into the period known as the Dark Ages, a time when corruption, religion and human power reigned. Rather than relationship with a living God, the churches now preached religion. Instead of the power of the Holy Spirit being manifest as the Gospel was preached, gatherings were marked by form and ritual. The Church of Jesus Christ once again needed reformation.

The word *reform* means "to improve or amend what is wrong, corrupt, unsatisfactory; to amend conduct or belief; to change to a better state or form; to improve by alteration, substitution or abolition; to cause a person to abandon wrong or evil ways of life or conduct; to put an end to abuses, disorders, etc.; to convert into another and better form; to change, alter; to bring a person away from an evil course of life." The Church of the Dark Ages needed reformation, so in 1517, God raised up a priest named Martin Luther who nailed the "95 Theses" to the door of the Castle Church in Wittenberg, Germany, and declared that "the just shall live by faith" (Romans 1:17). This launched the second reformation of the Church, the Protestant Reformation, realigning the Body of Christ with the Word of God.

In response, the Roman Catholic Church did not discern this God-ordained transition and resisted it. But the new Protestant Reformation built upon one ancient, shining light of truth within the Catholic Church—the Apostles' Creed—even as it separated itself from false, unbiblical teachings such as salvation by good works, indulgences and praying to Mary and the saints.

Bishop Hamon, C. Peter Wagner and others have declared that the Church is now in the beginning stages of the third reformation. For this reason we must discern the new season we are in, build upon the restored truths of previous seasons and embrace the new assignment for the new day. In his book *Prophetic Scriptures Yet to Be Fulfilled* (Destiny Image, 2010), Bishop Hamon tells us of the important transition season we are in and why:

> God's purpose for the First Reformation was to birth and establish the Church in all the earth. The purpose for the Second Reformation was to restore all truth and ministries back into the Church that were lost during the Dark Age of the Church.

God's purpose and timing is now for the Third Reformation to complete the restoration of all things and bring transformation to the nations and the kingdoms of this world until Revelation 11:15 becomes a historical fact.

He goes on to answer the question, What is Church reformation?

A reformation is a time when God makes a major shift in the Church to accomplish a specific purpose. There will be many times of refreshing, revivals and restoration movements during a Church Reformation. There are new orders, new grace, and new vision that give a new directive and goal for the Church to fulfill God's newly revealed purpose for His Church. A reformation brings a revolutionary change and separates the old from the new. Those who stay with the old order and refuse to accept the new become the main persecutors of those who become participators of the new reformation. It was that way in the first and second Reformations and will end up being the same for the Third Reformation.

Paul encouraged Timothy about the importance of having a strong foundation in the things of the Spirit so that he would be diligent always to be established in "present truth": "For this reason I will not be negligent to remind you always of these things, though you know and are established in the present truth" (2 Peter 1:12). One way to understand present truth is that it is the truth God is emphasizing at the moment. We need to discern the present truth of God's restoration so, like Solomon, we work with it and not against it.

Discerning the Disruptors

In times of building, restoration and reformation it is important not only to discern what God is doing but also to discern the strategies of the enemy to resist the building process.

At one point in our ministry God began to speak prophetically about a "paradigm shift." God was going to bring us into a new season in which everything would change. Our church was not going to look the same, as God was bringing us into something new. The leadership seemed in agreement with this word and began to seek God diligently about what the new season would look like.

As we endeavored to move forward, however, a spirit of division slipped in. Several leaders in the ministry tried to define and implement this new season, perhaps out of their own frustration. They began to make judgments of other leaders, Tom and me included, and began to spread their discontent.

One point of disagreement was their insistence that we were to shut down our prophetic ministry teams and move on to the "new thing." They said, "You pioneered that in an old season, but now God has moved on to something else." They did not properly discern God's order of spiritual authority or God's process of transition. They could no longer receive input from the other leaders on the team because they had moved out of alignment in their hearts—and in their mouths. As God began to bring our ministry into a time of multiplication and advancement, they resisted. Over time those leaders went elsewhere. But we experienced the fulfillment of God's word as He led us into expanded influence. He increased our church size and ministry potential as we moved into God's new season for us.

Any time God is moving in our midst and bringing advancement, excitement and acceleration, we should be mindful of those who come to disrupt. Many a move of God has fallen prey to wolves in sheep's clothing. Understand this: If God is moving, so is the enemy!

In the time of rebuilding the Temple after the Babylonian captivity, Cyrus the Great gave a decree that released the Jews from captivity and allowed them to return to their land, rebuild the Temple and restore the city. They returned and laid the foundation for the Temple. There was great joy and excitement as the promises of God for deliverance and restoration were actually happening right before their eyes.

But then, we read in the book of Ezra that the enemy conspired against this new building season. The adversaries in the land offered to help build the Temple, even saying they also sacrificed to God. But Zerubbabel and Jeshua told them they could not participate: "Then the people of the land tried to discourage the people of Judah. They troubled them in building, and hired counselors against them to frustrate their purpose all the days of Cyrus king of Persia, even until the reign of Darius king of Persia" (Ezra 4:4–5).

Zerubbabel, who was a governor of Judah and an apostolic type, and Jeshua, who was a priest and prophetic type, discerned the hearts and motives of the people of the land and the enemy's strategy for compromise. The Jews did not need idolaters helping to rebuild their holy Temple, even if they made false claims of following God. And even if they actually had made sacrifices to God, the Temple had been destroyed so those would not have been proper sacrifices. And it was questionable which god they were really sacrificing to.

When Zerubbabel rebuffed them, their true colors came out. They discouraged, troubled and frustrated the people of Judah until the building process came to a full stop. The new king after Cyrus issued a decree to stop work, shutting down the reformation process.

It is interesting that the titles of the two kings who stopped the building process show us what the enemy desires to do to resist forward advancement. The first was Ahasuerus, whose title means "I will be poor and silent." The enemy wants to cut off financial supply as well as take your voice, thereby paralyzing you in your progress. The second king who continued the resistance was Artaxerxes, whose title in Hebrew means "I will make the spoiled to boil." The enemy loves to stir things up!

History indicates that this second ruler was an imposter, posing as the son of Cyrus. He usurped the throne after the death of Ahasuerus, obstructed the rebuilding of the Temple and was eventually overthrown. We understand from this that the enemy often desires to rule as an imposter or usurper with illegitimate authority. He will resist and obstruct what God wants to build. We have been called to discern and overthrow every illegitimate rulership in the spirit realm and discern every work of resistance.

The spirit of resistance was at work during Israel's time of reformation. It caused a delay in the building of the Temple until the prophets Haggai and Zechariah prophesied and stirred the people to move forward once again (see Ezra 6:14). Today we must be aware that God is reforming and rebuilding His Church and that a spirit of resistance is attempting to bring confusion and delay. What broke the delay in the days of the second Temple? The leaders discerned the disruption, and prophets began to prophesy. Prophets break the stalemate of the enemy and cause God's purpose to advance.

Intellectual Awareness

A similar thing occurred when Nehemiah was overseeing rebuilding the wall of the city of Jerusalem. He discerned the false prophets who were sent to entrap him, to put him into a state of fear and to get him to sin. They wanted to thwart his assignment and set him up to fail so they could bring an accusation against him. This is the way the enemy works, but discernment uncovered the enemy's plans.

Nehemiah 6:12–14 tells us this:

> Then I perceived that God had not sent [Shemaiah] at all, but that he pronounced this prophecy against me because Tobiah and Sanballat had hired him. For this reason he was hired, that

I should be afraid and act that way and sin, so that they might have cause for an evil report, that they might reproach me. My God, remember Tobiah and Sanballat, according to these their works, and the prophetess Noadiah and the rest of the prophets who would have made me afraid.

Nehemiah said he perceived that God had not sent those false prophets. The word *perceived* is the Hebrew word *nakar*, which sheds light on the function of discernment. It means "to scrutinize, to look at intently (with suspicion implied), to disrespect, to ignore, to reject, to be strange toward, to pay attention to; the sense of physical apprehension through sight, touch or hearing; intellectual awareness." As we perceive the assignment of the enemy, we are able to avoid falling into his traps. If you have a sense of apprehension, God is probably giving you intellectual awareness and saying, "Pay attention to what I am revealing."

God wants to give His people the ability to perceive the false things that arise to get us off track in the midst of this reformation season. He wants to give us keen discernment to understand the working of the religious spirit, the false prophets and the spirit of resistance that would oppose the new thing. The Holy Spirit longs to empower us to have eyes to see as we rebuild and restore His Church, as well as rebuild and restore our cities. Jesus will build His Church and the gates of hell will not prevail!

ACTIVATION

Discern and identify any of the ways the enemy has resisted or disrupted God's building process in your life, business or ministry. Then prophesy what God says to that stronghold, break the demonic assignments of confusion and delay, and ask God for a strategy to advance.

7

DISCERNING
THE SPIRIT OF GOD

The Spirit of the LORD shall rest upon Him, the
Spirit of wisdom and understanding, the Spirit of
counsel and might, the Spirit of knowledge and of
the fear of the LORD.

Isaiah 11:2

My husband and I had the opportunity to visit St. Isaac's
Cathedral in St. Petersburg, Russia. We were on vacation and taking a tour of the city, which included this amazing
structure—the largest Orthodox basilica and the fourth largest cathedral in the world. It was built by Czar Alexander I
between 1818 and 1858. During the Communist revolution it
was turned from a house of worship into a museum. Today it
has been restored to look like a church, with altars, paintings
and statues of angels, apostles and evangelists. It continues to
be a tourist attraction, though a part is used for weekly services.

As Tom and I walked around looking at the beauty of the architecture and the artwork, we could not help but be saddened by the lack of representation of true Christian faith. It is a museum that commercializes the Russian Orthodox arm of Christianity, but without any imagery or focus on Christ's redemptive work. We commented on how empty the spiritual atmosphere seemed.

As we walked around we passed a small alcove and suddenly felt a rush of spiritual wind that caught us off guard. There was a tangible presence of God flowing out of that little alcove. We went to investigate and found a group of about twenty believers praying fervently. As we stepped into the room one of the individuals approached us to explain that they meet daily to pray that God will pour out His Spirit on this cathedral and on their city and bring revival.

That day I learned a lesson about discerning the presence of the Spirit of God.

Discerning His Presence

The gift of discerning of spirits is more than just distinguishing between demonic, angelic and human spirits. It is also vitally important that we are able to discern the presence of the Spirit of God and how He manifests Himself to us. There are times, as I travel from church to church, that I can sense a strong presence of the Holy Spirit among the people and other times when the spiritual atmosphere is dry, empty and even oppressive. I find it interesting that God's presence does not discriminate based on how beautiful the facility is or the size of the congregation. I have experienced God's tangible presence in some of the most hostile cities and in some of the most rustic churches. God wants to manifest His presence to those who are hungry and thirsty for more of Him.

My life was personally marked by the tangible presence of God. As a child I had a young friend who got very sick and died. This put a great fear of death in my heart. We were not churchgoing people, and the only prayer I knew was the one that started, "Now I lay me down to sleep. . . ."

I needed comfort in my soul, so I would go into my room, get down on my knees and begin to tell God what I was feeling. Suddenly, I would be surrounded by comforting warmth—like liquid love—and I knew He was there. My heart would beat faster, and I would be filled with joy. I knew He had come to hear what I had to say and to let me know I was not alone.

I continued to pray every night for the next nine years before I was ever presented with the Gospel and understood God's plan of salvation through the cross of Jesus Christ. Early in my walk with God I became dependent on His presence and learned to love it more with each passing year.

Even now, at any time, I can stop and close my eyes and think of Him and can feel that same surrounding presence, a stirring in my chest, a comforting warmth, and I know He is here. After all, my body is the temple of the Holy Ghost. He does not just come upon me when I call on Him; He lives in me, abiding at all times.

Accompanying Signs

In the Old Testament we find that the presence of God was easy to discern, as it normally came with accompanying signs. Rabbinical teachers often refer to the visible sign of God's presence as the *Shekinah* glory. This term does not appear in Scripture but in rabbinical texts, in which *Shekinah* means "the dwelling or setting of the divine presence of God."

Moses was a man who experienced the presence of the Lord in the burning bush as well as on the mountain that was covered with smoke when he received the Ten Commandments. As he led Israel out of captivity, the *Shekinah* presence of the Lord went with them, manifested as a cloud by day and a pillar of fire by night. Moses experienced the presence of the Lord when he pitched a tent outside the camp and called it the "tabernacle of meeting." Whenever he went into the tent a pillar of cloud would descend and stand at the entrance as Moses and God would meet together, and all the people would see this sign. These encounters with God caused Moses' face to shine with glory to the point that he had to keep his face covered from the people. Moses loved and was completely dependent upon the abiding presence of the Lord in his life.

In the times of Solomon the *Shekinah* presence of the Lord was once again seen with tangible signs. It did not take much discernment to know God was present when fire fell from heaven and consumed the meat laid on the altar of sacrifice. It did not take much discernment when the entire Temple was filled with a cloud of the glory of the Lord so the priests could not even stand to minister: "And it came to pass, when the priests came out of the holy place, that the cloud filled the house of the LORD, so that the priests could not continue ministering because of the cloud; for the glory of the LORD filled the house of the LORD" (1 Kings 8:10–11).

In the New Testament we do not usually see visible, tangible signs such as a cloud or a pillar of fire. Instead the Holy Spirit loves to manifest His presence through signs such as people being set free from oppression, healed in their bodies and minds, filled with the Spirit and speaking in other tongues. God's presence can be discerned in the stirring of emotions and at times even as a physical weightiness of His glory, as though someone has dropped a warm blanket around a person's shoulders.

Discerning God's Glory

The word *glory* is the Hebrew word *kabowd* and means "heaviness, weightiness (in a good sense), glory, honor, glorious abundance, dignity, splendor, brightness, majesty, beauty, desire, strength, power, portion, abundance, wealth, treasure; to prevail, to make rich." Moses cried out to the Lord, "Show me Your glory" (Exodus 33:18). He was crying out to see God manifest in majesty and splendor. He was crying out to see God's *Shekinah*, God dwelling with us. This is exactly what God did for us when Jesus came to the earth. John 1:14 (KJV) says that "the Word was made flesh, and dwelt among us, (and we beheld his glory, the glory as of the only begotten of the Father,) full of grace and truth." Jesus became the very manifestation of God's *Shekinah* joining heaven and earth.

God's glory is a manifestation of His Person, His presence, His power and His prosperity. When God's glory is present miracles happen, demons flee and supernatural answers are released. Glory is the demonstration of who God is as He interacts with the earthly realm. Glory is not just a shimmering cloud showing up but is actually a realm we step into and access all we need from the Father. God's glory changes things!

Make no mistake, God's cloud of glory still fills rooms and changes lives. My friends Mahesh and Bonnie Chavda have told the story (and I have seen the video) of a night during a Signs and Wonders Conference when a glory cloud showed up during their time of worship. On February 24, 2001, their ministry was meeting in a tent before they built their current facility. During worship a cloud of glory began to form over the congregation. There were particles in the cloud that caused different colors to be seen, including silver and gold. It was a sign to the people of God's manifest presence. When something similar happened at Bethel Church in Redding, California, Pastor Bill Johnson explained it by saying, "You can't invite God into your house and not have something outside of your box happen." It is when the "out of the box" happens that we must discern the presence of the Lord.

In the New Testament the word translated as "glory" is the Greek word *doxa*, which means "dignity, honor, praise, worship, splendor, brightness, majesty, a most glorious condition or exalted state." But interestingly it also means "opinion, estimate (whether good or bad concerning someone) judgment or view." It comes from the root word *doko*, which means "to think, to be accounted, to be of reputation, to be of an opinion." Hidden in the word for *glory* is an expectation to discern or have an opinion about what is taking place. It gives us a perspective about God's process as 2 Corinthians 4:17 (KJ2000) encourages us: "For our light affliction, which is but for a moment, works for us a far more exceeding and eternal weight of glory." We discern God's presence but also discern His process and His perspective.

Discerning the Mood of God

Not only do we discern God's presence; it is also important to discern His mood. There are times in corporate worship when the presence of the Lord is so strong the people drop to their knees or lie on their faces in reverence. There are times of laughter, dancing and joy and there are other times of holy awe, repentance and fear of the Lord. There are times when God is in the mood to go to war against His enemies and involves His people through corporate worship and prayer. Our God is a God of breakthrough and will often challenge us to rise up in faith and actively lay hold of that breaker anointing (see Micah 2:13). There are other times when God is in the mood to pour out love on His people, healing hearts, reviving our spirits. There are times when there is a tangible anointing for healing or miracles.

We must discern the mood of the Holy Spirit so we can cooperate with Him and flow with all He desires to accomplish in our midst.

Discerning the Move of God

When Jesus Christ came and walked the earth as a man, God initiated the greatest move of revival the earth had ever seen. This move of God was accompanied by powerful preaching, signs and wonders, healings and miracles. Yet many of the religious crowd of that day did not discern the move of God and actually opposed and resisted it. John 1:10–11 says of Jesus: "He was in the world, and the world was made through Him, and the world did not know Him. He came to His own, and His own did not receive Him." As a matter of fact, the religious leaders of that time accused Jesus, God incarnate, of having an evil spirit and said He was casting out devils by the power of Beelzebub (see Mark 3:20–22; Luke 11:16–19). They actually told the people that Jesus was out of His mind! They failed to discern that God Himself was with them.

The religious spirit will often rise up and accuse those who are moving forward in the outpouring or manifestation of the Spirit of God. We read in Acts 5 that the apostles were teaching and preaching the Gospel of Jesus Christ when the religious leaders got so angry they sought to kill them.

But one of the teachers, Gamaliel, a religious counsel member, was more discerning. He told the other members of the religious counsel: "I say to you, keep away from these men and let them alone; for if this plan or this work is of men, it will come to nothing; but if it is of God, you cannot overthrow it— lest you even be found to fight against God" (Acts 5:38–39). Any time God is moving and something new is happening we need to guard our hearts against resistance from the religious spirit.

Years ago we experienced a time of outpouring in our church services. We held special meetings with a guest minister who would preach on the anointing of refreshing and then lay hands on people to receive a touch from the Lord. Night after night people gathered to spend time in the anointed atmosphere.

Some would lie on the floor and laugh, others would cry. People were being touched and healed in their souls and their bodies. It was an amazing time of the tangible presence of the Lord, an outpouring of God's glory.

One evening the guest minister and his team began to read testimonies from people who had been touched by God in other meetings he had conducted. He asked for one of his team members to come read a particular testimony. That person began acting "drunk" in the Spirit: laughing and wobbling on the way to the platform and eventually falling to the floor, as the priests did in Solomon's Temple. One after another, different team members came to the platform and were not able to read the testimony because they ended up on the floor.

As I watched what was happening from the front row I was struck with the thought, *This looks really fake.* As each one came forward, it seemed the "manifestations" of the Spirit got more intense, and I got more upset. I was thinking, *The presence of the Lord has been so real. Why do they have to exaggerate it like this?* What I was seeing was definitely "out of my box," and I did not like it one bit.

Suddenly, the guest minister asked me to come up and read the testimony since his team had been unsuccessful.

I thought to myself, *Bless God! I am going to read that testimony!*

So I stood up and began to walk forward, ready to put an end to all the nonsense. When my foot touched the first step of the platform I felt a spiritual wind that I immediately recognized as the Spirit of the Lord. It knocked me off my feet.

At that point I realized I had seriously misjudged the situation! My predecessors on the platform were not faking it. There was an overwhelming power from the presence of God that made it impossible to stand. Some ushers came and helped me maneuver the rest of the steps, and I wound up leaning on the heavy podium. I could not stand on my own because the presence of the Lord was so strong. I did my best to read the testimony, punctuated by the laughter that I previously derided coming from my own mouth.

Needless to say, I ended up on the floor just like the people before me. I had misjudged the presence of God and the manifestations of the Spirit because it did not fit in my box of how I thought God should move.

Test the Spirits

When something begins to occur in our spiritual times of worship that is out of the box, God asks us to test the spirits to see if they are from God (see 1 John 4:1). How do we judge what is happening? We must judge by the Word and the Spirit. Here are some questions you can ask to help you determine whether or not a sign or occurrence is from God:

- Is it scriptural?
- Does it bring glory to God or draw attention to man?
- Does it bear good fruit in the life of the believer? Are believers changed for the good?
- Are people drawn to a deeper, more committed relationship with God?
- Is it sensual?
- Is it just pleasing to the soul or is it pleasing to the spirit?
- Does it bear witness in one's spirit?

If you sense something wrong in the spiritual atmosphere, you will need to determine why it feels wrong. I like to describe it as a "ping" in my spirit or a feeling in my gut. Sometimes what I am sensing can be simply immature or impure human actions. But, more seriously, I could be sensing something demonic that must be dealt with.

I was ministering in a church once that had a strong emphasis on dance and the arts. I love this expression of worship and was excited to learn that their dance team would be ministering. But as I watched them dance I had a sudden "ping" in my spirit that something was not right. Rather than stirring the presence of the Lord, I felt the dance was tainted by something very unclean. I did not want to be critical of the dancers. They were very talented and had an excellence in performance. Yet I could not get away from the feeling that something was off, impure and wrong. At times when I sense an unclean spirit I get nauseated, which happened that morning. The dance felt sensual. It was not so much the movements, but somehow there was a spirit behind the movements that was not the Spirit of God.

The feeling of being sick to my stomach persisted through the service until I got up to minister and had the people lift their hands and pray with me. Without mentioning the dancers I simply commanded every unclean spirit to go and asked God to purify our hearts and minds to prepare us to receive the Word of God. Immediately the sick feeling left, and the spiritual atmosphere lifted. It was almost as if a glaze came off the eyes of the people so they could see and hear God again.

I also prayed prophetically and decreed that God would expose every place the enemy was hiding to turn hearts away from His presence. I declared that God would expose the things that were impure and unclean and would open up our eyes to see His glory. Please notice that I did not rebuke the dance team publicly (though I did speak to the pastor privately about what I sensed). I did, however, take authority in the Spirit in such a way that any undiscerning congregation member would not have even known what occurred. But the prayer shifted the atmosphere and many people were touched by God, healed and prophesied over that morning.

Weeks later the pastor called to tell me that he had discovered that one of the dancers was in an illicit sexual relationship with one of the other dancers. Their sin was not just a private matter but was affecting the spiritual atmosphere of the entire church. One of them left the church, but the other one stayed to repent, get healed, delivered and counseled into restoration. Several years later that church became the gathering place for a mighty revival where the glory of God showed up in a powerful way.

Discerning the Anointing

First John 2:20 tells us we have an anointing from the Holy One. It goes on to encourage us that the anointing we have is real: "As for you, the anointing you received from him remains in you, and you do not need anyone to teach you. But as his anointing teaches you about all things and as that anointing is real, not counterfeit—just as it has taught you, remain in him" (verse 27 NIV1984). We know that God's anointing is real and that He uses people to administer that anointing to release His blessings and power to others. The problem is that God's pure anointing flows through flawed, imperfect people. We are the ones God has chosen to be His representatives in the earth and, let's face it, none of us is perfect, just forgiven. For this reason we must clearly discern soul from spirit (see Hebrews 4:12) to rightly divide the word of truth (see 2 Timothy 2:15).

Sadly in the Church some imitate the anointing, using personal knowledge to masquerade as prophetic gifting. We have also heard stories of ministers who preached the word with power, demonstrating miracles, signs and wonders, only to discover they were privately living immoral lives. Is it possible to sense the anointing of God and at the same time discern and distrust the person ministering? Can a supernatural gift operate through a person in an accurate manner when the person has disturbing issues or even sin in his life? These are oftentimes confusing matters when it comes to discernment.

Tom was given one of the most life-defining prophetic words of his life when he was sixteen years old. He received confirmation of his call to ministry and was hit by the power of God, which left him shaking on the floor. This life-changing prophetic word was spoken to him by a man who died of AIDS a few years later from living a secret homosexual lifestyle. It was an accurate word, but the vessel was flawed.

In times of revival and outpouring we must recognize that not everything that is happening is representative of God and His anointing. There was a large revival, for example, that was having impact on many lives. People were turning their hearts to God, getting healed, delivered and set free. There were even reports of the dead being raised. Several people from our church went and had their lives totally changed.

But my husband and I had checks in our spirits, gut reactions that made us very uncomfortable about promoting this revival in our church, though we could not deny that God was moving. We felt there were hidden things going on and prayed that they would be brought to light for the sake of the Body of Christ. After a time, it was discovered that the lead minister was involved in a sinful relationship that eventually destroyed his marriage. The revival had to be shut down as he submitted to a process of spiritual restoration.

It is very confusing when God seems to be moving and yet there also seems to be evidence of the operation of sinful human flesh. Remember: A little leaven leavens the whole lump (see 1 Corinthians 5:6). A tainting of impure, sinful human actions has the capacity to bring down a mighty move of God. Just because signs and wonders are occurring does not mean the life of the one ministering is pure or that his or her doctrines are sound. We must have the capacity to discern the Spirit of God and sound doctrine from that which is unhealthy, unbiblical, immoral or deceptive.

How Can These Things Be?

Bishop Hamon tackles this confusing issue in his book *How Can These Things Be?* (Destiny Image, 2015). He writes:

> Why does God work with ministers who are living a double life? . . . People ask, why would God confirm these ministries by working miracles, souls being saved or great financial prosperity? The fact is that God is not confirming their ministries at all, but a divine principle is at work here. Mark 16:20 gives the principle that helps us understand how these things can be. It says that after Jesus had spoken to the Apostles about preaching the gospel with accompanying miracles of casting out devils and healing the sick, He was received up into heaven and sat down at the right hand of God. And the disciples went out and preached everywhere, the Lord working with them and CONFIRMING THE WORD through the accompanying signs. . . . God does not work miracles, save souls or prosper a person to confirm the person or their ministry. . . . God confirms His Word with souls being saved and miracles of healing because the preacher preached God's truth of salvation and miracles, and someone received and believed the truth of God's Word and the truth set them free from sin and sickness.

Since we are living in unprecedented times of outpouring, refreshing, revival and reformation we must continuously guard our own hearts against these pitfalls as well as learn to discern when things are not pure. The good news is, this is one of the most exciting times in Church history as God is activating His anointing in and through believers everywhere and demonstrating His power in signs, wonders and miracles. His heart is that His people always pursue relationship with Him first and foremost, and then gifts and power will flow to touch the lives of others. As we are diligent to develop sensitivity to hear the voice of God, we put ourselves into a position to partner with God in a powerful way to cause His Kingdom to be advanced in the earth.

—— ACTIVATION ——

Each of us can live life in His presence and can sense His surrounding love at any time. I invite you to shut your eyes and still your natural senses for just a moment. Activate your spirit-man by praying in the Spirit for a couple of minutes, and ask God to let you know He is there. Then be still. Sense Him. Feel His warmth. Listen to His voice. Learn to discern the presence of the Lord in your life, and it will strengthen the reality of your intimate walk with Him every day.

8

DISCERNING ANGELS

Praise the LORD, you angels of his, you powerful warriors who carry out his decrees and obey his orders! Praise the LORD, all you warriors of his, you servants of his who carry out his desires!

Psalm 103:20–21 NET

I was asleep in a hotel room in Ypsilanti, Michigan, when my alarm rang. I hit the snooze button and snuggled back under the covers as I was thinking about a dream I had just had.

Suddenly, I felt a hand on my shoulder shake me hard and a loud voice said, "Wake up!"

This scared me and sent adrenaline shooting through my body as I sat straight up in bed. I knew immediately this was an angel. I did not see it with my physical eyes, but I knew it was sent to me for some divine purpose.

I said, "Wow, Lord, I thought I *was* awake."

The Lord replied, *Most of My Church thinks they are awake when they are still asleep. You need to wake up so you can wake them up.*

I knew the Lord was not just speaking of getting out of bed that day, but rather, that He wanted to awaken the Church from its spiritual slumber and bring the next Great Awakening in the earth.

Angelic Interaction

From Genesis to Revelation the word *angel* appears 289 times. In Hebrew the word *angel* is the word *malak*, which means "to dispatch as a deputy, a messenger, specifically from God; an ambassador." The Greek word translated "angel" is *angelos*, which also means "messenger, an envoy from God, one who is sent." Holy angels are sent by God with messages for mankind. Sometimes they appear in a vision (see Acts 10:3) or in a dream (see Genesis 31:11; Matthew 1:20). At times, they are obviously supernatural beings (see Judges 13:6). At other times they appear as regular men. Angels do not have a gender but nowhere in Scripture do angels appear in a female form, though culture often depicts them that way. Interestingly, whenever we are told of angels interacting with humans they always appear as male.

Though angels operate in the unseen realm on a constant basis, there are occasions recorded from Genesis to Revelation when angels step out from behind the veil to appear to humans (and in the case of Balaam, to a donkey). In the Old Testament angels appeared to Hagar, Abraham, Jacob, Moses, Joshua, Balaam, Daniel and the prophet Zechariah. In the New Testament angels appeared to Zacharias (the father of John the Baptist), Mary (the mother of Jesus), the women at the tomb, Cornelius, Ananias, Peter, Paul, Silas and John the Revelator, to name a few. These appearances span the old covenant and the new. With this much frequency of the topic in Scripture we need to understand that this is one of the ways God communicates and interacts with us prophetically.

I have a friend whose small son saw angels clearly with his natural eyes. They would travel to different churches, and she would ask him, "Do you see any angels? What are they doing?"

If the people were worshiping he would often describe the angels as worshiping with the people. If the people were praying he described the angels as spinning swords as the prayers and decrees were released. Once they were in a particularly dry church when she asked her son, "What are the angels doing?"

He looked around searchingly, looked up, then looked all the way to the back of the sanctuary and said, "They are just hanging out and talking in the foyer." If angels participate with us based on our actions I sure do not want those sent to co-labor with me just talking and hanging out!

Discerning the Unseen Realm

Scripture is clear about an unseen realm around us that is as real as what we can see with our natural eyes. One of the best examples of this occurs in 2 Kings 6 when the prophet Elisha was in a city called Dothan with his servant, and they were surrounded at night by the Syrian army.

You see, Elisha had been prophetically spying on the war council of the Syrian king. Every time he devised an ambush, Elisha would see it in the spirit and warn his own king not to fall into the trap. So the Syrian king sent an army to kill Elisha. When the servant got up early the next morning, he saw chariots and horsemen surrounding their city.

Elisha's servant panicked and said, "Oh, no! What are we going to do?"

Elisha responded, "Don't be afraid. Those who are with us are more than those who are with them." Then he prayed for his servant, saying, "Lord, open his eyes that he might see."

131

The servant's eyes were opened, and he saw that surrounding the armies of Syria were the chariots and horsemen of the Lord, His angelic host.

Elisha was right! The angels in the unseen realm outnumbered the armies in the natural realm. It was true in the natural realm that they were surrounded, but there was also a supernatural reality about their situation. The supernatural trumps the natural every time! Our prayer should be: "Lord, open my eyes so that I might see." When we are able to discern angelic and demonic activities in the supernatural realm we can properly position our faith and actions for the necessary breakthrough.

Cautions Concerning Angels

The supernatural realm is full of activity of both angels and demons. When Lucifer fell from heaven, he took one-third of the angels with him. These fallen angels became his demonic force by which he afflicts mankind. Two-thirds of the angels, however, did not rebel and remain at the command of the Lord.

Because angels were created by God, the holy angels and those that fell may actually look the same and, therefore, need to be discerned. Paul warned us of this when he said, "Satan himself transforms himself into an angel of light," and again said, "If we, or an angel from heaven, preach any other gospel to you than what we have preached to you, let him be accursed" (2 Corinthians 11:14; Galatians 1:8). Satan never comes to us with horns, wearing a red cape and carrying a pitchfork. No, he comes imitating true angels with a smile and deception.

Let me warn you: It does not matter how supernatural your experience is. You must discern any "angelic" encounter based on how the message aligns with the Word of God, by the behavior of the angel and by the discernment of the Holy Spirit—not by emotions or wonder of the mystical interaction.

Hebrews 1:14 says that angels are sent "to serve those who will inherit salvation" (NIV1984). In other words, they are sent to help us accomplish our missions here in the earth. They are powerful beings that can turn the tide in battle, but the Word of God cautions us to keep angelic interactions with man in alignment with God's purposes:

1. Angels are not to be worshiped, for they are only messengers of the Lord (see Colossians 2:18).

   We do not seek angels or angelic encounters; we seek the Lord and His Kingdom. We do not pray to angels; rather, Jesus taught us to pray to the Father. We are instructed that there is no mediator between God and man, except "the Man Christ Jesus" (1 Timothy 2:5). In Revelation, we read that on two occasions when John encountered an angel, he fell down and began to worship (Revelation 19:10; 22:8). The angel told him not to do that because he was just a fellow servant of the Lord. Any angelic encounter that causes one to worship an angel—and the action does not bring a swift rebuke—is suspect.

2. Angels are not ours to command; the Lord is the Captain of His hosts (see Joshua 5:15).

   We can ask God to send angelic help knowing He commands the angel armies as the Captain of the host. According to Psalm 103:20–21 we can decree His word and angels will respond: "Bless the LORD, you His angels, who excel in strength, who do His word, heeding the voice of His word. Bless the LORD, all you His hosts, you ministers of His, who do His pleasure."

3. Angels are sent on assignment from the Father to help us in the earth realm and are not here for our personal entertainment or friendship.

There is no place in Scripture that describes a person being in a friendly relationship with an angel to call on him at his will. When Jesus was tempted by Satan to cast Himself down from the pinnacle of the Temple, the discussion was focused on the ministry of angels (see Luke 4:9–11). The devil used the passage from Psalm 91 that says, "He shall give His angels charge over you, to keep you in all your ways. In their hands they shall bear you up, lest you dash your foot against a stone" (verses 11–12). Jesus refused to fall to the temptation to prove that angels would save Him.

4. We must not build doctrine based on messages from angels.

Second Timothy 3:16 tells us that "all Scripture is given by inspiration of God, and is profitable for doctrine." Angels may give direction, insight, battle strategies and instructions, but anything they communicate must align with the Genesis-to-Revelation Word of God.

Two major world religions base their false doctrines on supposed supernatural encounters with angels. The religion of Islam centers on supposed revelation Mohammed received from an angel that identified himself as Gabriel. This false angel gave him a whole new gospel, exactly as Paul warned against; therefore, we know this was not the angel Gabriel sent by God but, rather, a counterfeit sent by Satan to lead mankind astray. The second is the Church of Jesus Christ of Latter-day Saints, better known as the Mormon church. The doctrine of this false church is based on supposed revelation received by Joseph Smith from an angel named Moroni. These doctrines are contained in *The Book of Mormon*, which is also called *Another Gospel of Jesus Christ*. Neither of these religions is aligned with the Scriptures given by inspiration of God.

Understanding the Roles of Angels

Though there are warnings concerning how we interact with angels, we must understand that they are all around us and have a vital role in what is occurring in the earth. Angels are seen in Scripture fulfilling many different roles. There are some angels who have the assignment of worshiping around God's throne continuously. Cherubim and seraphim are continuously ministering to the Lord in heaven. Other angels have assignments that bring them into the earth realm, where they occasionally interact with people. Hebrews 13:2 challenges us to be hospitable to strangers, because they might actually be angels in our midst. The only angels that have been identified by name are Gabriel, Michael and the fallen angel, Lucifer. Other than these, we can only identify angels by how they function in their assignments. Here are various functions as defined in Scripture.

Prophetic Messenger Angels

Angels are seen most often in Scripture bringing prophetic messages from God to man. Remember, the word *angel* means "messenger," so this is a proper description of what these angels do. Gabriel is a messenger angel. He is identified four times by name: when he was sent to help Daniel understand a vision (see Daniel 8:16); when he gave skill and understanding about the future to Daniel as he was praying and seeking God (see Daniel 9:21–22); when he announced to Zacharias that his barren wife, Elizabeth, would have a child, who would grow to be known as John the Baptist (see Luke 1:11–20); and, most famously, when he appeared to Mary and told her she would supernaturally conceive a Child, "the Son of the Most High," and she would call His name Jesus (see Luke 1:26–38).

Prophetic messenger angels communicate God's plans and call men and women to align themselves with God's purposes. The first recorded instance of this mission is the angel who spoke to Hagar, the handmaiden of Sarah, announcing that her son, Ishmael, would become a great nation (see Genesis 16:7–11; 21:17). Messenger angels spoke to Abraham several times regarding the destiny of the nations that would come from his loins (see Genesis 22:15–18). An angel appeared to Moses out of the burning bush and spoke to him about his calling to deliver the people of Israel from Egyptian bondage (see Exodus 3:2). An angel found Gideon hiding in the winepress threshing wheat and called him to lead an army to deliver Israel from the hand of the Midianites (see Judges 6:11–12). An angel in human form visited the parents of Samson and told them her barren womb would be opened, and she would give birth to a deliverer (see Judges 13:17–21).

It is interesting that many of these angelic appearances signaled an era of deliverance that God was bringing into the land. As we are now in a prophetic time when God desires to deliver nations, we can expect similar angelic messengers to be sent to individuals called to work with His divine purposes in His *kairos* times in the earth.

Prophetic messenger angels are seen throughout the New Testament from the announcement of the birth of Jesus to rolling away the stone that sealed Jesus' tomb and announcing to the women who came to tend to His body that Jesus was not there: He was risen from the dead! There are also numerous accounts of angels bringing messages to the early Church apostles and leaders that help us understand the role of angels today.

God will use messenger angels to lead ministers to locations where they can reach the lost. An angel directed Phillip into the desert so that his path would intersect that of the treasurer who served the Queen of Ethiopia; the man received Christ and was baptized (see Acts 8:26). An angel also appeared to Cornelius, the unsaved centurion, and told him to send for Peter, who would tell him what to do to be saved (see Acts 10:3–7). God uses angels to orchestrate salvation for the lost.

An angel spoke to Paul when he was at sea in a storm and assured him that he would not die, nor would any of the 276 people aboard ship with him, for he had an assignment in Rome to come before Caesar (see Acts 27:23–24). Messenger angels will be sent at times to clarify spiritual assignments, just as the angel spoke to me that morning in my hotel room regarding my assignment to awaken the Church.

Warrior Angels

In Revelation we see a picture of a spiritual battle raging in the unseen realm: "And there was war in heaven: Michael and his angels fought against the dragon; and the dragon fought and his angels" (Revelation 12:7 KJV). Michael, one of God's chief princes or archangels, is seen fighting for God's cause.

This is also seen when Daniel received a vision and began to pray and cry out to God for answers. Gabriel brought answers to his questions, but he also gave a peek into what was happening in the spirit realm. Gabriel explained that as soon as Daniel began to fast and pray he was dispatched with the answers, but the prince of Persia (a spiritual principality) withstood him for 21 days. Michael had to come and engage in the battle so that Gabriel would be free to deliver his message to Daniel (see Daniel 10). This tells us that there are times when angels are sent in answer to our prayers but spiritual opposition tries to delay the answer. Michael is also mentioned in Daniel 12, which speaks of the last days and how at a time of great trouble he will stand for God's people and will deliver them. He is a mighty, warring angel sent to battle on our behalf.

We see other occasions in Scripture when warring angels are sent to bring judgment against God's enemies or the enemies of God's people. When David called for a census of Israel, God sent an angel who brought punishment and judgment on the land for three days but stopped him before he destroyed

Jerusalem (see 1 Chronicles 21:15). Again, when Jerusalem was besieged by the Assyrians in the days of King Hezekiah, God sent one angel down that killed 185,000 soldiers in the enemy's army and set the city free (see Isaiah 37:36). God will send angels to fight for cities and nations.

I once dreamed of angels called the Four Horsemen of Awakening and Revival. They were angels dressed in white and were linked arm in arm. They presented themselves to me as the necessary team to bring nations into their destinies of breakthrough, revival and awakening.

Upon waking I thought about these four horsemen. I knew that Revelation talks about four horsemen bringing death, famine, war and pestilence to the earth; these were not those angels. These were angels carrying hope, restoration and reformation to the earth. These four angels were linked arm in arm as a unified force with an assignment to bring awakening into nations.

Interestingly, the man preaching at the gathering being held the night after I had the dream, Greg Bailey (a modern-day prophet who heads up Christian International Australia and New Zealand), had us all stand and link arms together as a sign we were partnering with heaven—just as I had seen the angels linking arms in my dream.

He said it was the one-hundred-year anniversary of the World War I Battle of Gallipoli in which the ANZAC (Australia and New Zealand Army Corps) penetrated the Middle East. These brigades were called the "Light Horsemen." (He really had my attention then!) Though they were eventually pushed back at Gallipoli and suffered a horrible defeat, they went on to win a major, miraculous victory at Beersheba (meaning "the well of the oath or covenant") where eight hundred Light Horsemen, armed only with bayonets and a Bible, charged the guns of the Turks and Germans and miraculously overtook them.

Their bravery was so inspiring, some of the Turkish soldiers, the enemy, actually put down their guns and applauded the Light Horsemen forces. It was these armies, along with the British forces, who just six weeks later, took Jerusalem back after twelve hundred years of Muslim rule! The date of the Battle of Beersheba was October 31, 1917, the four-hundred-year anniversary of the birth of the Protestant Reformation.

There are hundreds of military testimonies from both sides of the battle for Beersheba in which soldiers reported seeing lights or "light beings" fighting alongside the Light Horsemen. Both sides saw angels mobilized on the field of battle. Some accurately recognized these as angels. Others mentioned seeing chariots and horses seemingly fighting from heaven with the ANZAC and British troops. These soldiers won the battle and liberated Jerusalem against impossible odds.

In addition, 1917 was a Jubilee year. As a sound of freedom was arising in the earth, the angel armies were sent to war to see a land set free. Heaven and earth worked in partnership to see Jerusalem released! As God's people arise, the angels are given orders concerning us (see Psalm 91). God's "Light Horsemen" are arising—heavenly horsemen who will fight for us and earthly horsemen who will rise up to take cities and bring liberty for the cause of Christ.

Angel Armies

As previously noted God has armies of angels in heaven who are fighting alongside Michael for the sake of God's people. God is identified 238 times in the Old Testament by the term *Lord of hosts*. This term actually indicates that God is the Lord of the angel armies. The word *hosts* is the Hebrew word *tsaba*, which means "a mass of people organized for war or a campaign, an army of soldiers or warriors." God has an army of warriors organized under His command to carry out His word. One of His names is Jehovah Tsabaoth—"the Lord of the Angel Armies." When we speak and decree words from God, He activates His angel armies to carry out His commands.

Tim Sheets, who holds the modern-day office of apostle, has written an incredible book on this subject entitled *Angel Armies* (Destiny Image, 2016) and has this to say about what these armies do in response to God's commands:

> It is time for the apostles and believers to begin affecting their regions with the Gospel, as angels under Holy Spirit supervision network with the church. They are moving now upon fresh Holy Spirit winds to assist the saints to do the same works Jesus did. They are flashing about as lightning. They are striking the enemies of King Jesus. Angels are bringing coals from the altar to cleanse iniquity and "purify the people of God." They are ambushing hell's forces. They are acting on prophetic words. They are enforcing the decrees of the saints based on Scripture. They are pushing out principalities, powers, might, and dominions from the dark side that have organized against our King. They are helping to organize the new Kingdom of Heaven event that is taking place now. Angels are at work releasing God activity into the remnant. They are working the harvest with us. They are assisting the Third Great Awakening that has now begun. They are connecting people, places, and activities through the Holy Spirit's campaign. They are assisting in the return of stolen property, sevenfold. They are connecting for miracles, building and activating God's wonders, creating and giving Holy Spirit signs— all clearly revealing confirmations.

God is calling His people to discern angels so that we can understand the movement of His angel armies in the heavens and in the earth. They have been sent to help us break through and win the battle.

Angels of Deliverance, Breakthrough and Protection

We noted earlier the verse that says, "He will command his angels concerning you to guard you in all your ways; they will lift you up in their hands, so that you will not strike your foot against a stone" (Psalm 91:11–12 NIV1984). An angel was sent to open prison doors for the early apostles (see Acts 5:18–19) and to deliver Peter from prison as well (see Acts 12:7–9). An angel was sent to shut the mouths of hungry lions when Daniel was thrown into their den (see Daniel 6:22). When Israel was fleeing Egypt an angel led them and also was their rearguard. The angel stood between the camp of the Egyptians and the camp of Israel to protect them and deliver them from Pharaoh's hand (see Exodus 14:19–20). Psalm 34:7 tells us that "the angel of the Lord encamps all around those who fear him," and Isaiah 63:9 encourages us that the "Angel of His Presence" saved Israel.

When we are in trouble we can ask the Lord to send angels of deliverance to help us, as this is part of their assignment from the Lord in the earth.

Ministering Angels

Angels are sent to minister to God's people on earth and to help us accomplish our spiritual assignments. Scripture says, "To which of the angels has He ever said: 'Sit at My right hand, till I make Your enemies Your footstool'? Are they not all ministering spirits sent forth to minister for those who will inherit salvation?" (Hebrews 1:13–14). This means angels will strengthen us (see Daniel 10:18), bring us new skills and understanding (see Daniel 9:22–23), explain revelation from dreams and visions (see Daniel 9–10; Zechariah 1:9) and encourage and comfort us (see Zechariah 1:13).

Angels can even feed us as they fed Elijah after the attack of Jezebel. He was able to travel forty days and nights on the strength of that supernatural food and get back on track in his mission to restore Israel (see 1 Kings 19). An angel even went with Elijah when he had to confront the king of Samaria (see 2 Kings 1:15). Angels have our backs and even provide moral support!

Angels can position us for prosperity: "The Lord will send an angel before you and prosper your way" (Genesis 24:40). An angel appeared to Jacob in a dream and gave him a prosperity strategy for separating from Laban (see Genesis 31:10–13).

Ministering angels keep us on the right path and help us get to our destination. When God was bringing Israel out of Egypt and into Canaan He said, "Behold, I send an Angel before you to keep you in the way and to bring you into the place which I have prepared" (Exodus 23:20).

Tom and I were once traveling in Eastern Europe and needed to catch a train in the large station at Prague. We were going to Vienna with first-class tickets, but could not figure out which platform to go to as we were not familiar with the train system and did not speak the language.

Suddenly a man walked up to us and said, "You go Wien [Vienna]."

Clearly we did not understand what he was saying, so he said it again.

"You go Wien. You go first class. Come."

And he grabbed our luggage and started walking. As we ran to keep up with him, he kept assuring us, "You go Wien. You go first class. Come."

There was no way that he could have known where we were headed. He led us to a train platform. A few minutes later a train pulled up for Vienna with the firs-class car right in front of us. He carried our heavy bags onto the train.

Tom tried to give him money for his help, but he declined. He stepped off the train to the platform, and Tom also stepped down to insist he take the money, but he was gone! It had been only one or two seconds. He had disappeared. We were stunned to realize God had sent an angel to get us where we needed to go.

The Tongues of Angels

First Corinthians 13:1 gives us this fascinating concept: "Though I speak with the tongues of men and of angels." One day I was praying in the Spirit when this verse stirred my heart. I knew that when we pray in tongues there are times we may be speaking in an earthly language. On the day of Pentecost people heard the Gospel preached in their own native languages after the disciples had been filled with the Holy Spirit and spoke in tongues. We had just witnessed a nine-year-old girl from Latin America who spoke no English get filled with the Spirit and speak in tongues in perfect English, praising God in her new tongue.

But on this day I realized that there are times when we could be speaking a heavenly language, one the angels speak, as the Holy Spirit gives utterance. Through our prayer languages the Holy Spirit might actually be issuing orders for the angels to carry out. The Holman Christian Standard Bible translates Psalm 91:11–12 as: "He will give His angels orders concerning you, to protect you in all your ways." Numbers 20:16 says that the people of Israel cried to the Lord for help, and He heard their voice and sent an angel.

Since that day I have activated people to pray in the Spirit with the express purpose of petitioning the Lord to send angelic help or breakthrough into a situation. It is amazing to hear the testimonies of miracles that occur when people ask the Lord to send angelic help.

God has always used angels to speak to His people prophetically, to protect, deliver and guide. In this season of awakening in the earth we should expect to hear of and even experience angelic interactions to assist us in breaking through and carrying out our missions. We must evaluate every angel encounter—not based on how supernatural it is, but rather by three crucial points: Does the message agree with Scripture? Does the angel give glory to God? Does the peace of God result from having been touched by heaven? As we learn to discern angels we will recognize the armies of heaven coming to earth to shift us into all God has ordained.

ACTIVATION

Take time to pray in tongues with a specific need in mind, petitioning the Lord to send angelic help to bring your breakthrough.

9

DISCERNING DEMONS

"Deliver us from evil."
Matthew 6:13 KJV

Tom and I were in Rio de Janeiro, Brazil, with more than a hundred youth one summer when we encountered a woman possessed by the devil. The young people were conducting a meeting in an auditorium on a college campus, and the leaders were stationed around the room to watch over the gathering and pray. I felt a demonic presence come into the room and began to pray that God would cause it to expose itself so we could deal with it.

A woman stood up, sat down, then stood up again and approached me. In broken English she said, "I no Christian; I voodoo."

At that time a translator approached my husband and me and began to converse with this woman in Portuguese. We discovered she was a voodoo high priestess. She had come on assignment to disrupt the meeting, but "something" made her come tell me who she was. She willingly accompanied us out of the meeting, where we found a place to pray for her and began to cast the devil out.

It was one of the most surreal experiences I have ever had, as several distinctly different voices spoke out of her, and her face contorted into different shapes. At one point the translator got frustrated with us because we were not waiting to let her translate what we were saying. I assured her the devil knew what we were saying.

Suddenly, the woman began to speak perfect English in a deep, dark voice: "Back off! She belongs to me! She has made covenant with me! Leave her alone!"

The translator's eyes got very big, and she nodded her head in agreement with us. The end result was that the woman broke her covenant with the devil, repented, and we cast him out. The woman received Jesus Christ as her Lord and Savior and was even filled with the Holy Spirit that night.

Dissecting the Discernment

The deliverance and salvation of this voodoo high priestess began with praying in the Holy Spirit, which then activated the gift of discerning of spirits within me. The only way I can describe the feeling is to say that it was an initial gut reaction that got my attention. As I continued to pray I felt a sense of unease, apprehension and even fear. There was nothing happening in the natural to provoke those feelings. When there is no reason for a feeling or emotion in the natural there is a pretty good chance you may be picking up something in the supernatural realm.

During the deliverance there were times when the woman would weep pitifully and act as if we were hurting her. Of course, we were not touching her physically; it was the demonic power that was inflicting pain. She would also say, "Why are you being so mean to me?" (in Portuguese). We were not speaking harshly. In a level voice of authority we continued to command the controlling spirit of witchcraft to come out of her and let her go. We discerned it was actually the demon that was crying out trying to get us to back off by manipulating our compassion for the woman and to feel sorry for her. Our translator at one point tried to get us to stop praying, saying we were hurting her. We explained that we were not hurting her; it was the demons.

Then the woman started screaming, this time not in pain but rather in rage. She looked at us with pure hatred and began to seethe as she mumbled under her breath. Again, we discerned that the woman herself was not angry—but the demon that had been controlling her life was furious. We had to discern these actions to know whether it was the woman talking or the demon. We continued to speak the Word of God, plead the blood of Jesus and command the demon to come out and let her go. Eventually first one, then many other demons came out of her, and she was gloriously saved. She willingly gave her heart to Jesus and asked Him to forgive all her sin and to break every covenant she had made with evil. Her face shone with the light of God's love and forgiveness. In one moment she was translated out of the kingdom of darkness into the Kingdom of God's dear Son.

The Devil Is Real!

Most of the time when people discuss the Holy Spirit gift of discerning of spirits the emphasis falls on discerning demonic spirits. As we have seen, it is also important to discern the Spirit of God, angelic spirits and human spirits. But the discerning of demons is vital to bring deliverance, breakthrough and blessing as well as to advance God's Kingdom in the earth. Oftentimes, discernment of demonic strongholds will be the key to territorial transformation.

147

Sadly, today, many Christians no longer believe in the reality of Satan or demons; surveys bear this out, as large percentages of Christians when polled say they consider Satan to be only a symbol of evil. One of the greatest tactics of the devil is to convince people that he does not actually exist!

Satan and the fallen angels are very real and evil to the core. Humanism has promoted the belief that the spirit realm does not exist, either for good or evil. It says, life is just what you make it and just what you choose with no external forces influencing you. Hollywood, on the other hand, has made a concerted effort to normalize witchcraft and occult practices with the presentation of nice witches and people who use their occult powers to do good. To be clear, all occult practices are evil and all demonic activity is wicked.

Demons are real spirit entities that have power to hold people captive and must be clearly discerned and dealt with in order for the fullness of God's freedom to be experienced. These supernatural beings are not figments of imagination; demons were a main focus of the earthly ministry of Christ as He came to restore mankind to the Father. He came to preach the Gospel of the Kingdom, heal the sick and cast out devils. One must be willing to deal with the devil, just as Jesus was, to have an effective ministry or to fulfill one's life and calling as a believer.

Jesus is clear that "the thief comes only to steal and kill and destroy; I came that they may have life, and have it abundantly" (John 10:10 NASB). He also tells us the devil is a murderer, a liar and the father of lies (see John 8:44). He wants us to understand that there is an enemy who seeks to take advantage of us, and that we must recognize his ways.

Satan's name means "adversary" and gives us insight as to his nature. The name *Devil* means "accuser or slanderer." He is also called *Abaddon* and *Apollyon*, which mean "Destruction" and "Destroyer" in Hebrew and Greek respectively (see Revelation 9:11). Satan is mentioned in the Old Testament as the one who stood against Israel and provoked David to sin by taking a census of Israel (see 1 Chronicles 21:1); as the tormentor of Job and the murderer of his family (see Job 2); and as Lucifer, one "who weakened the nations" (Isaiah 14:12).

It is clear from examining the earthly ministry of Christ that a big part of His mission was to confront and cast out devils and to restore people to relationship with God. Each one of the authors of the New Testament books mentions demons in some form. Satan is seen as the tempter (see Matthew 4:3–10), the one who steals the seed of the Word (see Mark 4:15), the one who afflicts people with sickness (see Luke 13:16), the one who hinders fulfilling spiritual assignments (see 1 Thessalonians 2:18), and the one who torments (see Matthew 4:24). Many times when Jesus or the disciples were healing the sick, Scripture says they first cast out devils or unclean spirits (see Luke 8:2, 36).

Know Your Enemy

One of the principles of waging an effective war is to know your enemy. Second Corinthians 2:11 warns us not to be ignorant of the devices or evil intent of Satan lest he gain an advantage over us. The entire story of the Fall of man in the Garden of Eden in Genesis 3 is the first time the devil is seen in Scripture, and we learn much about his nature and tactics from the scene. He appears as a conniving, deceptive serpent who has the goal of separating man from his fellowship with God. He does this primarily in three ways:

1. Satan questions the voice of God.

   "Hath God said?" One of the tactics of the devil is to put an individual in a place of confusion, doubting the word of God. He wants to assault God's word directly, and convince us, as he did Eve, that there are no consequences to our failure to believe and receive God's mandates. When Eve responded by saying she and her husband were not to eat of the Tree of the Knowledge of Good and Evil or they would die, the devil said in return, "You will not surely die" (Genesis 3:4). He was saying there would be no consequence for sin. But we know that sin separates man from God, which is why we need a Savior to forgive us so we can be restored to full fellowship with our Maker.

2. Satan questions the nature of God.

After giving the false promise that Eve could eat of the forbidden fruit and not die, the devil went on to malign the character of God. He told her that God was holding back from her and Adam, because if she were to eat of this fruit their eyes would be opened and they would "be like God" (Genesis 3:5). The enemy loves to mischaracterize God's nature. He loves to suggest that serving God will limit our lives, cheating us out of all the joys this world has to offer. This is, of course, opposite from the truth: It is only as we serve God that we can reach our highest potentials in life and enjoy the blessings that come from righteousness, peace and joy. Sure, sin has pleasure for a season (see James 5:5), but there is a reality of heaven and hell, salvation and damnation about which the devil wants to deceive.

3. Satan questions the nature of man.

One other tactic the serpent used to deceive Eve was questioning her created nature. He told her that if she ate the forbidden fruit she would "be like God." What is wrong with this statement? Genesis 1:26–28 says that when God created mankind we were created in His image, after His likeness. We were created to be like God! He put His nature inside us so we could be His ambassadors,

His representatives on planet earth. Everything He is was deposited into us in seed form. Tom likes to say His DNA was put into us—His Divine Nature Attributes. So when the devil came to Eve and said "God doesn't want you to be like Him," he perpetrated spiritual identity theft. Eve forgot that she already was like Him. Her true identity was that she was made in the image of God! She was created to be His daughter, His friend and His companion. This is why Jesus came to earth: to reconcile us to God, our Father, and to remind us who we really are. Demons will always try to separate us from our Father's love by getting us to question who God is, what He says in His Word and whom He has created us to be.

Evidence of Demonic Activity

When we begin to identify the presence of demonic activity, it is important to look at two opposite markers: the obvious and the obscure. Even with the obvious we have to ask that God remove the veils from our eyes, since we often ascribe merely natural human choices to strongholds rather than see the demonic influence behind them. Demonic activity is obvious in occult, witchcraft, false religious and idolatrous practices, which violate the First Commandment to have no other gods before the one true God. We see additional demonic influence when there is an abundance of violence, lawless action, greed and avarice, sexual immorality, perversion, addiction, oppression, tyranny, calamity and death. Any and all of these in a person's life or in a geographic territory can be demon driven.

Some of the more obscure workings of demonic activity have impact in ways that might not seem quite as evil as those listed above but are, nonetheless, wicked. Second Corinthians 4:4 reveals that Satan is the god of this world and seeks to blind the minds of unbelievers to keep the light of the glorious

Gospel of Christ from shining on them. These attacks are often so subtle and may have other aspects of humanity mixed in that discernment becomes vital to breaking the power of the demonic force. Some of the more subtle workings of Satan that are demonically assigned are: pride, unforgiveness, strife, rebellion, prejudice, depression, grief, insanity, sickness and infirmity, poverty, rejection, abandonment, all forms of fear, anger and rage, jealousy, envy and strife, to name a few.

Scripture tells us:

> If you have bitter envy and self-seeking in your hearts, do not boast and lie against the truth. This wisdom does not descend from above, but is earthly, sensual, demonic. For where envy and self-seeking exist, confusion and every evil thing are there.
>
> James 3:14–16

There is always the challenge to discern what is a work of the flesh, a human choice or a demonic attack. The truth is, you cannot cast out the flesh, and you cannot counsel a demon. Sin must be repented of and the flesh subdued, but demons must be cast out.

Do not let the fact that demons are constantly looking for ways to attack, affect and influence you in your life become a discouragement to you. This is the battle we must fight, but we war from a position of victory knowing that Jesus Christ already won the ultimate victory on the cross to bring forgiveness of our sin.

In his letter to the Ephesians, Paul explained it this way:

> You used to live in sin, just like the rest of the world, obeying the devil—the commander of the powers in the unseen world. He is the spirit at work in the hearts of those who refuse to obey God. All of us used to live that way, following the passionate desires and inclinations of our sinful nature. By our very nature we were subject to God's anger, just like everyone else.

But God is so rich in mercy, and he loved us so much, that even though we were dead because of our sins, he gave us life when he raised Christ from the dead. (It is only by God's grace that you have been saved!)

Ephesians 2:2–5 NLT

Christians and Demonic Powers

Christians have been redeemed and forgiven of our sins. But does that mean we cannot be affected by demons? Jesus, the very Son of God, was tempted by the devil. If He was tempted to fall into the devil's trap, we must be mindful that we are also vulnerable. Jesus told Peter that Satan desired to sift him as wheat, but for him to be encouraged because Jesus had prayed for him (see Luke 22:31–32). Paul admitted that he had a thorn in the flesh that he called "a messenger of Satan" who was sent to torment him (see 2 Corinthians 12:7). Paul repeatedly had to deal with issues in the Church in which demonic, sensual and false things had crept in to ruin their liberty in Christ. We are blind and deceived if we do not believe Satan would try to torment, harass and deceive us away from God's truth.

But can a Christian have a demon? There is no clear scriptural evidence about a Christian being demonically possessed, but there is certainly indication that a believer can be demonically oppressed. Whether the demon is in, on or around a person, we have clear authority from the Word of God that its power can be broken, and it can be cast out.

Years ago we launched our local church deliverance teams. Two pastors in our church, Bob and Sharon Parkes, have faithfully raised up and administrated those teams each week ever since. We have had people come from near and far, not only to receive a prophetic word (which is what our ministry has been known for) but also to receive healing and deliverance from demonic oppression.

The night we launched our teams we experienced a sign and wonder that helped us know God was working with us in this new endeavor. Pastor Sharon had just finished preaching and teaching about deliverance, so the congregation understood what Scripture had to say on the subject. She then invited the trained teams to come stand with her, and anyone who wanted freedom could come and be prayed for.

The first person to come forward was an older, frail-looking woman whom none of us had ever seen before. She walked up to Pastor Sharon and asked for prayer. She then leaned in to whisper something, not aware that she was speaking straight into Pastor Sharon's lapel microphone. The whole congregation heard what she whispered.

"Please just pray for healing and don't try to cast out any demons," she said. "I am a Christian, and I don't believe Christians can have demons."

Pastor Sharon just smiled and laid her hands on the woman. She began to pray: "Lord, I pray that You would bless my sister and that You would heal her body." But then the prayer changed: "And Lord I rebuke the spirit of death that is holding this woman captive, in Jesus' name."

When Pastor Sharon said those words the woman was suddenly picked up by an unseen force and thrown about fifteen feet backward! The ushers, who were in the process of coming to stand behind her, missed her, so they ran up the aisle to help her up. As they were picking her up a deep, loud, demonic voice came out of the woman and declared, "You can't have her. She is mine!"

Everyone who was in the building that night will never forget it! The woman had just announced that she was a Christian and that Christians cannot have demons. The next moment she was thrown across the room, and a demon spoke out of her.

Pastor Sharon walked over and in a calm voice commanded the spirit of death to loose the woman and go. She immediately went limp as the demon left her. She lay on the floor under the anointing of the Holy Spirit as Pastor Sharon then asked God to heal her body. The woman eventually got up and went home grateful for the prayer and ministry.

A couple of weeks later Pastor Sharon got a call from this woman. She explained that the night she came to our church she had just been released from the hospital and was being turned over to hospice care since cancer had spread throughout her body. The doctors gave her no hope of recovery and fewer than thirty days to live.

She was so impacted by the ministry she received she went back to her doctor insisting he run a new scan of her body. They humored her, believing she was in denial concerning her condition. She called to tell us that on that Friday night she was delivered from a spirit of death and that all cancer had left her body! Doctors were astounded and ran several more tests to confirm that all cancer was gone. She came to our church several times over the years to give this testimony. Doctors had given her less than a month to live but she lived another eight years. When she went home to be with the Lord, she did not die of cancer, for God had delivered and healed her.

Called with Authority

Christians have been given a mandate from the Holy Spirit to rise up in the fullness of the authority given them by Christ. Jesus declared,

> "These signs will follow those who believe: In My name they will cast out demons; they will speak with new tongues; they will take up serpents; and if they drink anything deadly, it will by no means hurt them; they will lay hands on the sick, and they will recover."

> Mark 16:17–18

We have a mandate to move in the power of the Holy Spirit. These verses do not declare that all these signs, including casting out devils, are to be performed only by pastors or full-time ministers but rather by all believers. This is part of the inheritance Jesus Christ purchased for us by His blood shed on the cross. It was a foundational part of the first-century Church, which brought cities into transformation, and it is a necessary, vital anointing for each and every Christian to walk in today.

Though this verse tells us we can "take up serpents," I do not believe it is referring to "snake handling." Granted, that interpretation could be valid, considering what occurred with the apostle Paul when he was shipwrecked. He went to gather sticks for a fire. Among the sticks was a snake that bit him, but he did not get sick or die. It was a sign of God's power to those on the island who witnessed this. It is also a bit of a warning to us that when the fire of God comes, the spiritual snakes wake up! The enemy begins to cause things to get stirred up to bite and cause harm. But just as we saw in the story of Paul, the snakebite cannot hurt us when we are anointed and appointed by God.

A more accurate understanding of this verse can be found in the Greek words. The word translated "take up" is a Greek word that means "to lift up and take away, to remove." The word *serpents* is the Greek word *ophis*, which indicates not just the snake but also "an artful, deceiving, malicious person, especially Satan." So this portion of the verse, which reads "they shall take up serpents," could mean that we have been authorized to take up and remove Satan himself!

Jesus told His disciples what He was authorizing them to do as they ministered to the people: "Then He called His twelve disciples together and gave them power and authority over all demons, and to cure diseases. He sent them to preach the kingdom of God and to heal the sick" (Luke 9:1–2). He gives us power and authority over all demons, as well as the power to cure disease and to heal the sick, all while preaching that the Kingdom of God has come.

If you are a believer, this is what Jesus has called you to do. Some might say, "Well, I don't have that gift." Jesus says clearly that it is not about having a special gift; it is about being a believer.

Pushing Back

The idea of confronting and casting out devils can be a bit intimidating since these spirits do have power. But we need to know that we have been authorized by the power of the Holy Spirit to extend God's Kingdom in the earth by pushing back the gates of hell. The gates of hell cannot prevail.

The devil, however, will do his best to fill people with fear in order to keep them from using their anointing to discern and deliver. Bishop Hamon likes to say, "You can't make a peace treaty with the devil."

Before you think, *I would never do that*, I can assure you that many people are concerned that if they cast out demons, the devil will come back and attack their kids, their finances or their health. The devil tries to bring people into a peace treaty by saying, "If you leave me alone, I will leave you and all you love alone." But remember, you would be dealing with a liar! He will try to attack all those areas of your life anyway.

There is absolutely no scriptural principle that authorizes the devil to retaliate against one who casts out demons; rather, we have been given all authority over all demons. As a matter of fact, God promises that if there is retaliation against Him, He will swiftly and speedily return the retaliation on their own heads (see Joel 3:4, 7). Jesus promises that as He gives us power over all the power of the enemy, nothing shall by any means harm us (see Luke 10:19). We must break our peace treaty with the devil and rise up to the call to confront him and cast him out.

Overcoming Fear

When I first began discerning and exposing demonic assignments, I had a dream that showed the devil trying to intimidate me. In the dream God showed me a demonic spirit that was subtly attacking our ministry. When I exposed his plan, he looked at me and said he was going to come back and kill me. In the dream I was terrified but knew I had done the right thing. Then Tom and Bishop Hamon came and stood on both sides of me and said, "Don't worry, we will protect you."

When I woke up from this dream, I knew the devil was threatening me, trying to get me to shut down the gift of discernment or to back off from exposing him. But the promise from the dream was clear: If I do what I am called to do, I will be protected. My earthly spiritual covering would protect me, but it was also a promise from God that He would protect me. Isaiah 54:17 assures us: "'No weapon formed against you shall prosper, and every tongue which rises against you in judgment you shall condemn. This is the heritage of the servants of the LORD, and their righteousness is from Me,' says the LORD." In the New Testament we are further empowered with these words: "For God has not given us a spirit of fear, but of power and of love and of a sound mind" (2 Timothy 1:7).

The enemy will use fear to shut down our gift of discerning of spirits. But the good news is that we have power over all the power of the enemy. James 4:7 encourages us with these words: "Submit to God. Resist the devil and he will flee from you." If you have struggled with fear, you can submit yourself to God, resist the devil and renounce every partnership with fear and be free. Pray this prayer of deliverance with me:

*Heavenly Father, I thank You that You have not given me
the spirit of fear but of love, power and a sound mind. I,
therefore, repent of and renounce fear and every work of
darkness. I submit myself to You and break the power of
all fear off of my life. I command it to leave me now, in
Jesus' name. I pray that if I have in any way shut down
the gift of discerning of spirits because of this fear, that
You will now restore the full operation of the gift and give
me wisdom and understanding as I discern. I declare that
I will have no peace treaty with the devil but will be bold
and courageous to discern his workings and cast him out.
Thank You, Lord, for freedom! In Jesus' name, Amen!*

--------- ACTIVATION ---------

Remember: We war from a position of victory. These steps can
help you resist the enemy:

1. Pray and ask the Lord to show you any area of your life,
   family, business, ministry or area in which you live that
   the devil has been robbing, afflicting or affecting you.
2. Ask God to open your eyes to the specific evidence of
   the devil's intrusion, identifying demonic spirits and
   spiritual assignments and any ungodly agreements, decrees or vows that may be empowering them.
3. Submit yourself to God, meaning repent if there is any
   sin or ungodly belief allowing the devil's actions.
4. Then resist the devil through making your stand for
   righteousness, freedom and truth, decreeing that his
   power and authority have been broken by virtue of
   the shed blood of Jesus. Take your spiritual authority
   and verbally break the enemy's power and assignment
   against you. This is also a good place to make a decree

of the restitution the enemy owes you. Exodus 22:7, for example, says, "If the thief is found, he shall pay double." Decree a double portion restoration.

5. Scripture then tells us the devil will flee, so command him to do so, in Jesus' name.

10

DISCERNING
THE HUMAN HEART

> For the word of God is living and powerful, and
> sharper than any two-edged sword, piercing even
> to the division of soul and spirit, and of joints and
> marrow, and is a discerner of the thoughts and in-
> tents of the heart.
>
> Hebrews 4:12

For more than thirty years our church has held a weekly "Friday Night School of the Holy Spirit" in order to have an amazing time of worship, to hear the word of the Lord and to facilitate prophetic ministry. One night years ago, toward the end of the time of worship I saw a handsome, nicely dressed man come into the back of our sanctuary. He began to lift his hands to worship and seemed to be enjoying the spiritual atmosphere.

Something inside of me, however, was suddenly very angry. When I looked at the man, I felt an overwhelming urge to go hit him and tell him to leave our church! Of course I did not do either of those things—and proceeded to beat myself up for being so judgmental and critical.

What is wrong with me? I thought. *What kind of pastor/ prophet has those kinds of thoughts in the middle of an anointed time of worship? I must need some sort of deliverance!*

As the service continued, Tom held a prophetic activation in which he invited a young woman to come up and sit in a chair while everyone prayed and asked the Lord for a prophetic word for her. People began to line up to share what they sensed God saying.

This man got in line, and once again I felt a surge of anger. The closer he got to the front of the line, the angrier I became. The man gave the young woman a good, positive word and returned to his seat. Something was apparently wrong with me. He seemed like a nice guy. He had a nice smile and gave a good word. I definitely needed deliverance!

On the way home from church I shared my thoughts with my husband. Tom often coached me about keeping a right heart whenever I discerned issues about people. He would remind me that the prophetic gifts are given for edification, exhortation and comfort (see 1 Corinthians 14:3), not for the purpose of judging and becoming critical or angry. He wanted to help put my discernment into the perspective of the heart of God toward the person and show how God wanted the person set free. He has always been very wise, compassionate and motivated by mercy toward people.

That night he told me that the man had spoken to him to say he would be joining our church. This was going to be a real growth experience in discernment for both of us.

The man did, in fact, join our church. He attended every gathering. He came to prophetic training sessions and seemed to connect well with others. I was constantly repenting of my bad attitude toward him and praying that God would show me

His heart toward the man. It was a real struggle, as my initial reaction to him remained unchanged.

After he attended our church for a month, we discovered that he had sexually seduced three different women in our congregation and had manipulated them into giving him large amounts of money. When this came to light I thought, *I should have hit him and thrown him out of the church that first night after all!* Obviously that would not have been the correct response, but Tom and I both realized God had shown me that the man was a wolf in sheep's clothing and a danger to the flock. I remembered the earlier prophetic word I had received, that God had called me as a watchman and had anointed me to see the snake and see the wolf. My strong reaction to him was not an immature response while learning to operate in my gift but rather God stirring an extreme response to get my attention.

Hebrews 4:12 (KJV) tells us that "the Word of God is quick, and powerful, . . . and is a discerner of the thoughts and intents of the heart." The word *discerner* is the Greek word *kritikos*, which means "skilled in judging, tracing out and passing judgment on thoughts and feelings."

This is the most challenging area of operating in spiritual discernment. How can we discern what is going on in the heart and mind of a person and continue to walk in love? Sure, there was a demonic influence present with this man, but his actions and choices were calculated and purposefully deceitful. When Tom confronted him about what he had done, the man gave a sly smile, shrugged his shoulders and said, "So what are you going to do about it?" He was not in the slightest bit repentant. At that point my mercy-loving husband wanted to punch him and throw him out of the church. Instead, he told the man he would never be welcome at the church again and that we would publicly warn our congregation about him. The man disappeared from our area from that day forward.

False Brothers

Years ago a woman joined our church and seemed to go out of her way to bless Tom and me. She brought us gifts, gave us money to go out to dinner and volunteered to watch our children so we could go on a date. I did not feel comfortable with this woman but was working really hard not to be judgmental with my discernment, so we received her gifts but did not leave our children with her.

During the first month she was in our church, fifteen different intercessors came to us at different times stating they had major red flags of discernment about this woman. They said that whenever she was present they had strong warnings about her in their spirit, and each one expressed concern because she was trying to get close to us and our children.

When I asked the intercessors if they observed any negative or concerning behavior, no one seemed to have anything bad to say about her. She seemed to be a considerate, sweet woman. But something was definitely off in the spirit. Tom and I prayed together that whatever was hidden would be exposed without causing anyone any harm and that, if possible, we could help the woman be set free. This is often how we pray when we discern something in the spirit that has no tangible evidence in the natural.

Within a week this woman was involved in arguments, contention and accusations with others in the church. She asked to meet with us and demanded to know why we would not allow her to help with our children. She told us angrily that she was sent to us, and we were not allowing her to fulfill her calling. This actually made me even more uncomfortable. We explained that we did not know her well and would not be leaving our children with her.

This previously sweet, considerate woman suddenly flew into a rage. I am not sure who sent her to help us with our children, but I am pretty sure it was not God. She left our church that day, and we never saw her again.

The apostle Paul lists "false brothers" as one of the dangers he dealt with in ministry (see 2 Corinthians 11:26 NIV 1984). False brothers could have been those who were not believers who were infiltrating the early Church to disrupt and cause confusion from within. Or false brothers could have been true brothers in Christ who had corrupt, ulterior motives and hidden agendas to lead people away from appointed leaders so that they could promote themselves or some false doctrine, or lead people into sin.

Paul, noting the danger from these false brothers, mentioned them again in his letter to the Galatians:

> And this occurred because of false brethren secretly brought in (who came in by stealth to spy out our liberty which we have in Christ Jesus, that they might bring us into bondage), to whom we did not yield submission even for an hour, that the truth of the gospel might continue with you.
>
> Galatians 2:4–5

Sadly, false brothers were not just a danger to the early Church; they continue to plague churches all over the world today. False brothers have crept into the Church in Communist China, for instance, and exposed underground congregations to the government. Other hostile Communist nations, as well as Islamic-dominated cultures, often send spies into churches in order to harm Christians. Many believers and leaders have been imprisoned as a result. At other times witches or occultists attend churches regularly with the intention of casting spells, causing confusion and stirring up accusations and division.

But, as I suggested above, it is not just non-believers who spy on and disrupt the Church. It is a particular challenge to know how to respond properly when one discerns a false brother or sister in Christ—especially if the true picture is not demonstrated in the person's behavior. Paul said that when he discerned people were false he did not yield to their religious shackles "even for an hour," or as the Message translation says, he did not "give them the time of day." He understood the temptation to be distracted by trying to correct and corral the false brothers or appease or argue with their religious manipulation. Instead, Paul did not allow those who were false to interrupt the mission of preaching the truth of the Gospel. Sometimes the tactic of the enemy through false brothers (or sisters) is to wear out the minister with endless controversy. Paul warns not to give in to it.

Because there has been so little teaching on the subject, when people discern something is out of order or false with a fellow member in the Body of Christ they either do nothing with the revelation or they do the wrong thing. The result is that many people have completely shut down the gift of discernment and blocked their revelation receptors so as to not be burdened with knowledge they feel incapable of handling. Rather, believers should be endeavoring to understand how to receive and properly process the voice of God in discernment so the Kingdom of God may advance.

What to Do with What You See

When God reveals something to a believer through discernment, He also wants to give a strategy of what to do with what you see. Here are seven guidelines you may use to help you process things you discern so as to walk in balance and integrity with your gift.

Embrace the Gift Knowing That Jesus Operated in Discernment

Jesus was the most prophetic man ever to walk the earth. He always saw the big picture and was always aware of what was happening in both the spirit realm and the natural realm. He also had an amazing ability to discern the thoughts of people's hearts and to respond in such a way as to give people a chance to open their hearts and embrace who He truly was, though He also recognized He was challenging their religious mindsets. Jesus set an example for us to discern the thoughts and even evil intentions of the human heart:

> And some of the scribes were sitting there and reasoning in their hearts, "Why does this Man speak blasphemies like this? Who can forgive sins but God alone?"
>
> But immediately, when Jesus perceived in His spirit that they reasoned thus within themselves, He said to them, "Why do you reason about these things in your hearts? Which is easier, to say to the paralytic, 'Your sins are forgiven you,' or to say, 'Arise, take up your bed and walk'? But that you may know that the Son of Man has power on earth to forgive sins"—He said to the paralytic, "I say to you, arise, take up your bed, and go to your house."
>
> Mark 2:8–11

The word *perceive* is the Greek word *epiginosko*, which means "to know, to feel, to become thoroughly acquainted with, to recognize." Often when we suddenly discern something is not right, there is a knowing or a feeling that causes us to recognize the wrong thoughts or actions.

Again we see Jesus operating in discernment to recognize what was in the hearts of the religious leaders of the day:

> So they watched Him, and sent spies who pretended to be righteous, that they might seize on His words, in order to deliver Him to the power and the authority of the governor. Then they asked Him, saying, "Teacher, we know that You say and teach rightly, and You do not show personal favoritism, but teach the way of God in truth: Is it lawful for us to pay taxes to Caesar or not?"

But He perceived their craftiness, and said to them, "Why do you test Me? Show Me a denarius. Whose image and inscription does it have?"

They answered and said, "Caesar's."

And He said to them, "Render therefore to Caesar the things that are Caesar's, and to God the things that are God's."

But they could not catch Him in His words in the presence of the people. And they marveled at His answer and kept silent.

Luke 20:21–26

In this case, the word *perceive* is the Greek word *katanoeo*, which means "to observe fully, to discover." Jesus operated in discernment and never fell into the traps of the Pharisees. His discernment always allowed Him to be one step ahead of them in their schemes. He did not resist the Holy Spirit's insight or knowledge; He embraced the gift. He discerned the plan and purposes of heaven and His assignment in the earth. He discerned the thoughts of people. He also discerned the operation of demons and cast them out.

If you feel as though you have resisted the operation of the prophetic gift of discernment in your life, pray this prayer with me:

Lord, I repent of resisting the gift of discernment given by Your Holy Spirit from operating in my life. I recognize that there were times I did not understand the revelation I received and either did nothing or did the wrong thing as a result. Forgive me for any past mistakes I have made, and please restore the full function of this gift in my life for the benefit of Your Kingdom and the blessing of Your people. Let me be more discerning—just like Jesus. Amen.

Study the Subject of What You Have Discerned

Throughout this book you will find numerous stories in which I discern something then seek out greater understanding from the Word of God and other resources in order to comprehend what God is showing me.

Once I had a dream in which the enemy was chasing me trying to take a key from me. I knew the key would unlock the strategies for victory in our new season. When I woke up I asked the Lord what the key was.

I did not hear an answer. Then in a prayer time at church one evening one of our ministers came to me and said, "God told me to tell you, you have the key." So I had the key but did not know what it was.

The next morning Bishop Hamon called to say he had had a dream. In the dream the Lord said, *Makkedah is the key*. This sent me to study the word. I found it in Joshua 10—in the story of Joshua defeating the five Amorite kings at a place called Makkedah. Each of these kings represented a spiritual force that was withstanding our forward advancement. It gave us the strategy we needed to break through into our new season, and it came as I pressed in to study the Word of God.

Realize That Discernment Is Not Based in the Soul

Though God may at times help us recognize our discernment by stirring our feelings or emotions, we must also realize that discernment is based in the spirit not in the soul. Discernment is a function of the spirit, not of what we see with our natural eyes or hear with our natural ears. We cannot judge a person or situation based on how things look and call it "discernment." Remember, the prophet Samuel was able to discern prophetically that Jesse's oldest son, Eliab, was not God's choice for king, even though he looked and acted the part. Instead, Samuel discerned that the much younger son, David, was the one God had chosen. We might be tempted to look at the outward appearance, but God looks at the heart (see 1 Samuel 16:7).

Prophetic insight comes from our spirit man, which connects to the Holy Spirit. For this reason we must be careful not to discriminate based on our own opinions, experiences or cultural points of reference and then call it discernment. We must be careful not to take up a personal offense against someone and then draw the conclusion that we are discerning something demonic.

At one time, for example, I began to notice that I often had an emotional reaction of fear and mistrust whenever I got around men who wore beards. I realized that there was nothing wrong with a man wearing a beard, yet I had a strong, uncomfortable feeling that persisted. As I prayed about this I realized the connection to my soul (remember the soul is the mind, will and emotions). When I was a child, I was sexually abused by a man with a beard. Though God had healed me, apparently there was a trigger in my soul that still needed to be touched. I offered this broken place to the Lord and invited His healing power. I no longer have a soul reaction in this area.

We must be careful not to judge others' actions or behaviors and then form the opinion we are discerning something demonic in their lives. Immature actions in others are not necessarily evidence of demonic influence. Perhaps someone comes across as bossy and controlling; this does not automatically mean that that individual is controlled by a Jezebel spirit. Perhaps he or she had a painful childhood, which has caused some insecurity. That person might now be overcompensating by trying to create security through controlling others.

We must continually ask the Lord to help us look past the fruit a person is manifesting in order to see the root. It is easy to discern fruit, but it takes spiritual eyes to see the root that produces the fruit. Ask God to help you divide between what is soul and what is spirit.

There are times, however, when God will use feelings, emotions or even physical responses to stir discernment. When you get one of these responses for no apparent reason, with no prejudice about the situation, it very well might be discernment from the Holy Spirit.

I met a minister, for example, a man whom our organization was considering for ordination. He seemed to have a strong ministry, but when I met him I felt sick to my stomach. I was uncomfortable to the point of feeling unsafe when I was around him.

I mentioned my reaction to the leadership team, not wanting to speak against the man or destroy his reputation but feeling this was the responsible action to take so we could pray together. As we prayed, we spoke a decree that anything hidden that needed to be revealed would be made known to us in a way that did not harm anyone. Within weeks, the man confessed to being involved in an adulterous affair, which was apparently not his first.

That was what I had been discerning. The man submitted to a restoration process and is still happily married and serving the Lord in ministry today.

Recognize That Discernment Can Become Clouded

A woman joined our church and seemed excited about being a part of our prophetic ministry because she felt she had a strong gift of discernment. After being with us for a couple of months she came to speak with Tom and me about things she was discerning that concerned her. According to her, our staff was controlling, our worship leader was controlling, her "life group" leader was controlling, and, as a matter of fact, Tom and I were both controlling. And Bishop Hamon was controlling as well.

Her solution was for us to put her in charge of several of these areas and groups. She believed that God had called her to come to our church to straighten us all out! Obviously, she was seeing the world through her own issues and calling it discernment. She was unhappy because she was not the one in control. We only reinforced her judgment that we were controlling when we declined to give her a position and instead tried to help her see her own heart.

A little story illustrates this point. There was once a young boy who decided to play a trick on his grandfather. While his grandfather napped on the couch, the boy took some Limburger cheese (the super-stinky cheese) and put a tiny bit in his grandfather's mustache.

When he woke up from his nap, he sniffed and said, "Wow, this room stinks!" He walked around the house and sniffed and said, "Wow, this whole house stinks!" So he went outside and walked around the yard and sniffed and said, "Wow, this whole world stinks!"

The moral of the story is: When the whole world stinks, it is probably something under your own nose.

If we are not careful we begin to see the world through glasses that are tinted with our own issues. God might be showing you something about yourself, yet you think your word of discernment is for everyone else. This is a common prophetic pitfall. Romans 8:7 tells us that "the carnal mind is enmity against God." Proverbs 16:18 says that "pride goes before destruction, and a haughty spirit before a fall." Pride will corrupt discernment; humility allows us to hear God's voice clearly with an open heart. If you have a pattern of discerning the same thing over and over about others, my challenge to you is to check that this is not something under your own nose.

We need also to recognize that hearing the voice of the Lord in discernment is not a sign of being super-spiritual or being some sort of spiritual giant who is smarter and more discerning than others. Remember, Balaam's donkey was more discerning than Balaam and saw the angel in the path before Balaam did. Also remember the demons discerned and identified Jesus as the Son of God before any of the disciples did (see Matthew 8:29). James wrote: "You believe there is one God. You do well. Even the demons believe—and tremble!" (James 2:19). Humility and accountability are key to spiritual health and clear discernment.

Guard Your Heart from Being Judgmental or Critical

I have been blessed to be mentored by Bishop Hamon and Tom, who are two of the most mercy-motivated men I know. Their leadership styles exude love, mercy, benefit of the doubt and second chances. This has been invaluable to me as I have grown in operating in my prophetic gift of discernment and has provided a balance to challenge me not to become judgmental or critical, which quite honestly was my tendency in my early days. I had strong emotions attached to what I discerned about people and would have to be reminded that anything I discerned was a tool given to help people walk in love and be set free. Love and mercy must be a priority to walk in healthy discernment.

Paul prayed for the church at Ephesus that God would grant them the spirit of wisdom and revelation (see Ephesians 1:17–18). This is imperative for keeping a proper perspective when sensing dark or demonic things in the lives of others. Though God gives the ability for each one of us to draw on both wisdom and revelation, in every team, including marriages, some people are stronger in wisdom and some are stronger in revelation. It takes both wisdom and revelation to process prophetic discernment correctly. My strength of prophetic revelation is more life-giving and powerful when it works together with my husband's strength of wisdom. Revelation without wisdom is dangerous, and wisdom without revelation becomes dry and religious. I needed his wisdom, and he needed my revelation.

Romans 11:22 tells us to "consider the goodness and severity of God." God is both good and severe. It has been interesting to see in my own marriage, as well as in other marriages and various teams, that God will often pair a person who is more merciful in demonstrating the goodness of God with a person who is more righteousness- and justice-oriented and demonstrates more of the severity of God. I have already told you that my husband is the more mercy-motivated one, so you now know I come from the other direction. My personality leans more toward seeing things in terms of black and white: It is either black or it is white. But Tom tends to see things in terms of gray. When I make a decision I have a tendency to make more of a snap decision from my gut, whereas he considers all angles and options before deciding. Neither is right; neither is wrong. There are benefits and blessings to both approaches. We actually make a great team!

The problem is that if we are not careful we begin to judge each other because we do not think or process things the same way. We spend our time trying to get the other person to think as we do rather than celebrating our differences. Sometimes when I would discern something strongly and share it with Tom his love and mercy would kick in, and I would feel as if he did not hear or believe what I was saying. When I defended what I was seeing or sensing, he felt I was not hearing him or receiving his wisdom. We had to learn to appreciate our different perspectives and to realize that we were stronger and the discernment was clearer when we worked together. Through the years I have grown in wisdom and Tom has grown in revelation, which has made each of us even stronger.

During my growth period, I often felt defeated for not having a greater heart of love and mercy. I struggled with negative or harsh feelings toward others. One day I read Proverbs 31:26 about the virtuous woman: "She opens her mouth with wisdom, and on her tongue is the law of kindness." Then I read Micah 6:8, which says, "He has shown you, O man, what is good; and what does the LORD require of you but to do justly, to love mercy, and to walk humbly with your God?"

I cried out to the Lord, "Please let me love mercy," to which the Lord replied, *Jane, you do love mercy . . . when you are the one who needs mercy.*

This broke something in me that was harsh and judgmental. It enabled me to walk in clear discernment but also to have a deep heart of love and mercy toward others. I realized that I had been delivered and changed so that others could be delivered and changed.

We must realize that people are not our enemies. We do not wrestle with flesh and blood but with principalities and powers and spiritual forces (see Ephesians 6:12). Jesus' heart is to set people free. Note also that a person is not a demonic spirit. In other words, a person is not "a Jezebel" or "an Absalom," though an individual can be influenced by those dark powers. It is our job as Christ's ministers to pray for clear discernment and for keys to set them free.

Operating with a merciful heart does not mean, however, that we ignore a standard of righteousness. The man that I discussed earlier who was a wolf in our church was not repentant and, therefore, was not extended mercy but rather justice. Leaders need to know when it is time for mercy and when it is time to implement a standard of justice. Paul was not afraid to confront an unrepentant sinner and have the church elders turn someone over to Satan for the destruction of the flesh for the saving of the person's soul (see 1 Corinthians 5:5). This seems harsh, yet mercy was the motivator. "Mercy triumphs over judgment" (James 2:13).

Guard Your Heart from False Responsibility

As I was learning how to process all the revelation information that came from having the gift of discernment activated in my life, I felt overwhelmed and worn out. I wanted to stop the flow of what I was seeing, hearing and sensing because I felt burdened by the responsibility of the revelation.

One day I heard the Lord say to me, *Jane, I called you to see the snake and see the wolf, not kill the snake and kill the wolf.*

I realized that I was carrying false responsibility to solve all the issues I was discerning. I was being driven by a feeling of having to fix what I discerned was wrong. God reminded me that I was not the Savior; He was.

We are called to bear one another's burdens (see Galatians 6:2), so how do we do that without crossing the line into false responsibility? We realize that we are taking on false responsibility when we start taking responsibility for other people's sins, mistakes, actions and choices, and carry a burden of emotion that crushes the soul. We begin to believe that it is solely our job to pray people out of their problems. This can result in hyper vigilance and an inability to rest. It is the trap of the enemy to wear us out! When we find ourselves striving and pressing in our own strength, we need to stop and give the burden to the Lord and take His yoke upon us to enter into the rest of faith (see Matthew 11:28–30).

If you have found yourself carrying a burden of false responsibility I invite you to pray this prayer with me now:

Heavenly Father, I thank You for giving me spiritual eyes to see the things I need to see in order to extend Your heart to others and to advance Your Kingdom in the earth. I repent and ask You to forgive me for carrying burdens You have not asked me to carry. Forgive me for not trusting You with my life or the lives of others and for striving rather than resting in Your love. I lay my burden down at the foot of the cross. I release these individuals to You and ask that You place Your light yoke of peace upon me and give rest to my body and soul. Thank You for taking care of all that concerns me. In Jesus' name, Amen.

See It, Say It and Pray It

When we discern something we do have a responsibility to do something with what we see. We need to see it, say it and pray it.

SEE IT

Define the discernment as clearly as you can and write it down. Ask the Lord to clarify what He is requiring of you. What is your God-given responsibility? Maybe He simply wants you to be aware of the situation so you can make it a matter of prayer.

SAY IT

God might ask you to share your concerns with others. At our church we encourage people to write out what they are discerning and give it to someone on the leadership team through a note or email. A corporate meeting or church service is not usually a good time to share a dream, vision or word of discernment with your leaders; they need time to process, pray about and strategize regarding what you have shared. Each leader has a different way for this information to be submitted. But the key is to submit the word to the leaders, and then leave it with them to deal with in their own way.

I caution you against trying to dictate how the leaders respond to your discernment or how they deal with the situation. Once you share it with them, it becomes their responsibility to carry. Do not worry if your leader does not affirm your discernment. Leaders might not see what you see in the way you see it, but then again you might not know what they know—the process something or someone is in.

Speaking as leaders of a local church, Tom and I take this kind of information seriously, but we do not always see things the way the intercessor does. We value it, however, because quite often others share pieces of the puzzle that help us see the whole picture about what is happening in the spirit realm.

If you believe God is asking you to speak to the person you are receiving revelation about, it is usually best to submit what you are sensing to a leader first and to ask yourself the following questions:

1. What is my position in this relationship? Am I in a place to help this person? Or am I in a place to pray that no hurt comes to the individual or others, and that those who are better positioned to help also see the problem?
2. Do I have a voice of influence to speak what I see? Can I speak it in a way that edifies without judgment or condemnation?
3. If not, is there someone else I am to share with? Or do I just continue to pray?
4. What is my responsibility in this matter?

If the leader feels it is appropriate for you to share the matter you have discerned with the person, it is good to have a leader present as witness to the conversation. What you will be sharing is discernment, but it is also a prophetic word. Having a trusted witness present protects not only you as you give the word but also the person receiving the word. It is helpful to write out the matter you have discerned so that you can give the person a copy to pray about as well. In this situation it is important to do as Tom always advises: "Take the accusation out of the conversation, and you will have communication."

Pray It

You have a personal responsibility to pray about what God shows you. If you know a trusted intercessor or leader who can pray with you about the matter, that can be very helpful. Scripture tells us that two are better than one (see Ecclesiastes 4:9). Be careful, however, about sharing with others—in the guise of prayer—what you discern about someone. Never use a time of group prayer as a gossip line to spread negative information. Love covers a multitude of sins (see 1 Peter 4:8).

Warning! If what you are sensing is against the leaders or the direction the leaders are taking, be very careful how you proceed. This is not "prayer-meeting material" but something that should be navigated carefully and privately.

God will use the prophetic gift of discernment to help you set people free, to protect the Body from false brothers and to extend His love and mercy.

— ACTIVATION —

Is there a person in your life right now about whom you have uncomfortable feelings and about whom you are wondering if you are discerning something? Examine your sensing in light of the following:

1. Is there any possibility there is something about the person or his or her personality that you might be reacting to in your soul rather than in the spirit?

2. Pray and ask the Lord to show you how He sees the individual. If there is bad fruit being manifested, ask God to show you any root in his or her life that might be producing the wrong fruit so you can pray for healing and deliverance.

3. Examine your heart to be sure you are not forming judgments against the person or carrying false responsibility.

4. If after examining your own heart you feel that you are discerning that this is a false brother or sister, or that the individual has something demonic operating in his or her life, first see it: Clarify the matter as best you can and ask the Lord what your responsibility is. Then if necessary say it (share it with a leader). And be sure to pray it—follow through with prayer until you feel God's plan is accomplished.

11

DISCERNMENT AND SPIRITUAL WARFARE

For we do not wrestle against flesh and blood, but
against principalities, against powers, against the
rulers of the darkness of this age, against spiritual
hosts of wickedness in the heavenly places.

Ephesians 6:12

Thirty-five years ago God moved our ministry to a pristine
area of the panhandle of Florida. We were surrounded by
nothing but pine trees and beautiful white sand beaches. But
after a while we noticed something else was here—an entrenched
territorial spirit of poverty. There were no stores, no development, no progress. People opened businesses and then went
bankrupt. People built houses and had them go into foreclosure.
A spiritual force was locking up our area. We organized prayer
walks, undertook spiritual mapping and called for fasting and

prayer. We saw small breakthroughs but no substantial change in the area.

In 1997 Chuck Pierce gave our ministry a word that said, "In three and a half years I am going to give you a revelation to unlock the wealth and destiny of this region."

Sure enough, three and a half years later I was praying and seeking God about the spirit of poverty that seemed to be holding our territory captive. I was crying out asking the Lord why we were failing to see a transfer of wealth into our region.

God answered me, *It's because of Isaiah 65:11.*

I looked up the verse: "You are those who forsake the LORD, who forget My holy mountain, who prepare a table for Gad, and who furnish a drink offering for Meni." I discovered that Gad and Meni were Babylonian gods. Gad was the god that locked up wealth, and Meni was the goddess that locked up destiny. Wealth and destiny! I wrote extensively about these two demonic spirits in my book *The Cyrus Decree* (Christian International, 2001).

I pulled out Chuck's word and realized, as three and a half years had passed, that this was the key to unlock our region. I did some study to understand how these strongholds were affecting our area so we would know how to pray and repent on behalf of ourselves and our land. We called our leaders together to strategize, called our church to a time of prayer and fasting, then met to do strategic level warfare about this issue. We worshiped, prayed and released decrees to unlock God's created purpose for our land.

We saw immediate breakthrough as people in our church began to get contracts, new jobs, inheritance money that had been withheld and overall increase. Our church finances doubled because the people were breaking through. Within eighteen months our territory went from being one of the poorest counties in Florida to being named one of the richest real estate markets in the continental United States! Chuck's word to us and this clear discernment enabled us to tear down the stronghold of poverty and release prosperity in the region that continues to this day. A new season opened through discernment and spiritual warfare. Not only were the people of our church liberated, but the people of our territory reaped the natural and spiritual blessings as well.

Understanding Spiritual Warfare

Mankind was created in the image and likeness of God (see Genesis 1:26). Everything that He is, we are, in seed form (see 2 Peter 1:4). God is Jehovah Rapha so we have the spiritual DNA of the Healer in us. He is Jehovah Jireh so we have the spiritual DNA of the Provider in us. He is Jehovah Sabaoth, the Lord of the Angel Armies, so we have the spiritual DNA of the Warrior in us: "The LORD is a man of war, the LORD is His name" (Exodus 15:3). Our God is a warrior; therefore, we are warriors, too!

After God created mankind He charged us with exercising dominion over the earth: "Be fruitful and multiply, fill the earth and subdue it and have dominion" (Genesis 1:28). The word *dominion* means "to subjugate or to rule over." We are called to bring the earth, and all that is in the earth, under subjection to the rulership of the King of the universe and to see His Kingdom extended in the earth. God placed mankind here to become His Kingdom ambassadors, His delegated authority, to enforce His Kingdom rule.

But as we know, mankind fell into sin and lost our Kingdom authority to rule. This is why Jesus came to earth. Yes, He came to restore man to right relationship with God through the shedding of His blood for the forgiveness of our sin. But He also came to restore us to our original created purpose so we could operate as God's ambassadors once again. When Jesus came to earth He demonstrated this dominion to us by casting out devils, healing the sick, confronting religious spirits, walking on water, even prophesying to cities (see Matthew 23:37; Luke 10:13–15; 19:41). He preached the Gospel—not just the Gospel of salvation but also the Gospel of the Kingdom (see Matthew 4:23). He declared the Kingdom of God is not coming some day but has come to us now (see Luke 17:21). In order to see God's Kingdom established, He would have to subdue the works of the enemy: "For this purpose the son of God was manifested, that He might destroy the works of the devil" (1 John 3:8).

When Jesus died on the cross He "disarmed principalities and powers, making a public spectacle of them" (Colossians 2:15). The Passion Translation says it this way:

> Then Jesus made a public spectacle of all the powers and principalities of darkness, stripping away from them every weapon and all their spiritual authority and power to accuse us. And by the power of the cross, Jesus led them around as prisoners in a procession of triumph. He was not their prisoner, they were his!

So if Jesus won the battle against all demonic forces, principalities and powers, why do we still need to operate in discernment for spiritual warfare today? Because even after Jesus' victory on the cross we are told to give no place to the devil (see Ephesians 4:27) and to resist the devil (see James 4:7) because our "adversary the devil walks about like a roaring lion, seeking whom he may devour" (1 Peter 5:8).

Ephesians 6:11 directs believers to "put on the whole armor of God, that you may be able to stand against the wiles of the devil." The word *wiles* is the Greek word *methodeia*, which is where we get the word *methods*. This Greek term means "trickery, deceit, cunning arts, craft, to lie in wait" and describes the current action of our enemy. Paul wrote the believers in Thessalonica that he would have come to visit them but Satan hindered him (see 2 Thessalonians 2:18).

Make no mistake: The devil is still active in the earth, post-crucifixion and resurrection. There is still a devil we must contend with—but Jesus assures us He has already won the victory over Satan. We are called to enforce that victory by continuing the work of casting out devils and pulling down strongholds, extending His Kingdom dominion everywhere we go! This involves contending with the forces of darkness: "The kingdom of heaven suffers violence and the violent take it by force" (Matthew 11:12). The New International Version (1984) says, "The kingdom of God has been forcefully advancing, and forceful men lay hold of it."

Executing Written Judgments

Psalm 149:6–9 gives us the basis for this forceful advancement:

Let the high praises of God be in their mouth, and a two-edged sword in their hand, to execute vengeance on the nations, and punishments on the peoples; to bind their kings with chains, and their nobles with fetters of iron; to execute on them the written judgment—this honor have all His saints.

In his book *Silencing the Enemy with Praise* (Parsons, 2012), Robert Gay explains our current call to spiritual warfare in the scenario of a courtroom. He writes that a criminal is brought into a courtroom, tried and convicted. Then it is the bailiff who handcuffs him and executes the written judgment:

The act by the bailiff is the execution of the judgment that is written. The judgment or sentence by itself will not do the job. Someone must see to it that the judgment is executed or carried out. . . . Spiritually speaking, a judgment and a sentence have been pronounced on the devil. . . . That sentence, or judgment must still be executed. We (the church) are the bailiffs in God's great courtroom (the earth) where He sits as judge. Our praise binds the devil just as a police official handcuffs a criminal. Praise incarcerates him. The praises of God have divine power to execute the judgment decreed over the enemy. The devil is a convicted criminal and God has a warrant out for his arrest. What are we going to do about it? Let us, as the church of God, arise with praise in our mouths, as we execute His judgment upon the powers of hell.

This is spiritual warfare: to discern the actions and activities of our convicted enemy, and enforce the judgment that was written against him when Jesus won the victory over death, hell and the grave.

Empowered with *Dunamis* and *Exousia*

When Jesus walked the earth He explained what we could expect in dealing with the devil: "Then He called His twelve disciples together and gave them power [*dunamis*] and authority [*exousia*] over all demons, and to cure diseases. He sent them to preach the kingdom of God and to heal the sick" (Luke 9:1–2). He delegated His Kingdom authority to all of His disciples when He said, "Behold, I give you the authority to trample on serpents and scorpions, and over all the power of the enemy, and nothing shall by any means hurt you" (Luke 10:19). We have been given Kingdom power over all the power of the enemy— and he is not allowed to retaliate against us!

The Greek word *dunamis* is most frequently translated "power." It refers to the force of the Holy Spirit filling the life of the believer. It is the power to move into the supernatural and to operate in the miraculous. It is an anointing for breakthrough against every opposing force, including the use of spiritual violence, to defeat a foe. Our struggle is not against flesh and blood but against dark spiritual powers.

Jesus also gave us authority—*exousia*. This means "force" as well, but this force is described as "superhuman delegated influence or jurisdiction, a magistrate." It is a governmental term regarding our call to rule with the spirit of liberty, freedom, strength and power. Jesus was repositioning His Church to be rulers and legislators through divinely delegated and imparted *dunamis* and *exousia*—spiritual power and superhuman delegated authority—forces greater than any other force in the earth.

The Struggle Is Real!

It was for this reason the apostle Paul wrote that we must "fight the good fight of faith," for we wrestle "against principalities, against powers, against the rulers of the darkness of this age, against spiritual hosts [armies] of wickedness in heavenly places" (1 Timothy 6:12; Ephesians 6:12). This speaks of a hierarchy of demonic forces with which we contend in order to advance God's Kingdom. Paul makes clear that we are not battling or wrestling with people but with these dark spiritual forces in the unseen realm.

We noted earlier the reference in Scripture to spiritual warfare being waged in the heavenly realm against a principality named the prince of Persia (see Daniel 10:13). The angel Gabriel said this demonic prince withstood him, so the angel Michael joined in the battle. This was a demonic spirit ruling in the heavens over the land of Persia, whom Michael and Gabriel had to contend with in order to break through his control and deliver God's message to Daniel. The warfare began the very day Daniel prayed and asked for help and continued for 21 days. Daniel's fasting and prayers were the fuel that ignited the force of the angels in battle.

As he delivered his message, Gabriel told Daniel that he had to go back to fight against the prince of Persia alongside Michael, but that then the prince of Greece would arrive. Historically we know that Greece conquered Persia. It seems that once the dark principality over the land of Persia was defeated and driven out, a new principality was waiting in the wings. Principalities and demonic powers are real forces that set up structures to try to control nations. The good news is there are more with us than are with them (see 2 Kings 6:16)!

Jennifer LeClaire, in her book *Waging Prophetic Warfare* (Charisma, 2016), speaks about this concept of wrestling. She writes:

> We are not wrestling people: we are wrestling the enemy's unseen Special Forces assigned to derail our destiny. According to the KJV New Testament Greek Lexicon, the Greek word translated as wrestling in this verse refers to "a contest between two in which each endeavors to throw the other, and which is decided when the victor is able to hold his opponent down with his hand upon his neck." The devil wants to put you in a stranglehold. In the wrestling world, a stranglehold is an illegal hold that chokes the opponent. Merriam-Webster calls it a "force or influence that chokes or suppresses freedom of movement or expression." If the wrestler doesn't break free from the stranglehold, the lack of blood or air can cause him to black out. Translating this to our spiritual realities, the enemy wants to choke the Word of God out of your mouth so you can't wield the sword of the spirit or pray. He wants to choke your revelation of who you are in Christ and your authority over him. The enemy wants to counter the work of the blood of Jesus and the Holy Spirit in your life so you will sideline yourself.

The struggle is real, not imaginary. We are contending in a spiritual war for the sake of our families, our churches, our cities and our nations. As Paul traveled to spread the Gospel he often met opposing forces, both in the natural and in the spirit, yet he exclaimed: "Now thanks be to God who always leads us in triumph in Christ" (2 Corinthians 2:14). Remember, this was Paul who suffered shipwreck, beatings, stoning and all manner of persecution, yet he declared that God always gave him victory. Even in persecution he realized he was winning a victory against the forces of darkness and expanding the cause of the Gospel of the Kingdom in the earth.

Sometimes discernment means catching God's perspective in the midst of spiritual battle.

Spiritual Weapons of War

In order to wage a spiritual war we must employ spiritual weapons. The apostle Paul explained this concept:

> For though we live in the world, we do not wage war as the world does. The weapons we fight with are not the weapons of the world. On the contrary, they have divine power to demolish strongholds. We demolish arguments and every pretension that sets itself up against the knowledge of God, and we take captive every thought to make it obedient to Christ. And we will be ready to punish every act of disobedience, once your obedience is complete.
>
> 2 Corinthians 10:3–6 NIV1984

In *God's Weapons of War* (Chosen, 2018) Dr. Hamon writes:

> We have entered an offensive war that will not end until Jesus personally leads His army of saints in the final battle. Now is the time that saints must know their weapons of war and how to use them. . . . Pastors and all fivefold ministers must now function as drill sergeants and generals diligently training saints as soldiers who know how to fight as warriors in the army of our Commander in Chief.

He continues:

> We have an arsenal of offensive weapons . . . the sword of the Spirit, the name of Jesus, high praises, a shout of faith, tongues,

prophetic acts and apostolic decrees. I have led numerous nations in warfare using the Church's greatest corporate weapon, the shout of faith, which explodes in the demonic spirit realm like an atomic bomb in the natural. Many ministers have testified of major changes and shifts in the nation after our acts of pulling down strongholds. Our weapons of warfare are mighty in God for pulling down the strongholds of Satan.

Here are nine of the most powerful offensive weapons God has given us to win Kingdom victories.

The Weapon of the Power of the Word

Each of the weapons we fight with must be grounded in the written Word of God. Remember that the sword of the Spirit is the Word of God (see Ephesians 6:17). It is the only offensive weapon in the description of spiritual armor. In addition, God's Word is quick and powerful and sharper than any two-edged sword (see Hebrews 4:12). The word *sharper* comes from a Greek word that means "to cut by a single stroke, decisive and keen." When we discern that a spiritual battle is underway, we can speak God's Word and take the enemy out in a single stroke.

At one point, when the apostles were beaten and threatened, their prayer was to speak God's Word even more boldly and do signs and wonders (see Acts 4:29–31). The apostles wielded the sword of the Spirit against the enemy of fear, threats and even death. When we speak God's Word with boldness it becomes a spiritual force, a weapon that withstands darkness. Jesus is the Word of God (see John 1:1) so when we speak the Word, we have all the power of the risen Christ backing us.

The Weapon of the Power of the Blood of Jesus

Revelation 12 describes the strategy of those who were victorious in their battle with Satan: "And they overcame [the enemy] by the blood of the Lamb, and by the word of their testimony, and they loved not their lives unto the death" (verse 11). Our entire warfare is based on the victory Jesus obtained through the shedding of His blood for our sin:

> Inasmuch then as the children have partaken of flesh and blood, He Himself likewise shared in the same, that through death He might destroy him who had the power of death, that is, the devil, and release those who through fear of death were all their lifetime subject to bondage.
>
> Hebrews 2:14–15

The power of the blood of Jesus has redeemed us from every sin and broken the power of every curse. The blood of Jesus destroys every work of the devil and empowers us to enforce that victory on earth as it is in heaven.

The Weapon of Prayer

According to James 5:16, "The effective, fervent prayer of a righteous man avails much." The Amplified Bible, Classic Edition, says it this way: "The earnest (heartfelt, continued) prayer of a righteous man makes tremendous power available [dynamic in its working]." General George Patton, who led the U.S. military offensive to liberate Europe during World War II, made this observation: "Those who pray do more for the world than those who fight; and if the world goes from bad to worse, it is because there are more battles than prayers."

One of the most powerful aspects of transformative warfare prayer is when believers pray in the language of the Holy Spirit. When we engage in praying in tongues to wage spiritual warfare, we are assured of releasing a pure flow of the heart and mind of God, even with groanings that cannot be uttered (see Romans 8:26). The Passion Translation puts it this way: "The Holy Spirit rises up within us to super-intercede on our behalf." As we pray in tongues, angel armies are mobilized to carry out the decree of the Spirit. Praying in tongues builds faith in the believer (see Jude 1:20) and produces a spiritual force of *dunamis* that brings transformation (see Acts 1:8).

The Weapon of Praise

God ordained praise not because He needs to be praised, but because we need to praise Him. Praise is a weapon in the life of the believer. Psalm 8:2 says, "From the lips of children and infants you have ordained praise because of your enemies, to silence the foe and the avenger" (NIV1984). Psalm 18:34 says, "You've trained me with the weapons of warfare-worship; now I'll descend into battle with power to chase and conquer my foes" (TPT).

When we combine worship and praise with the prophetic voice of God we level a punishing blow to our enemy as God rises to fight for us in response:

> The voice of the LORD will shatter Assyria [the enemy]; with his scepter he will strike them down. Every stroke the LORD lays on them with his punishing rod will be to the music of tambourines and harps, as he fights them in battle with the blows of his arm.
>
> Isaiah 30:31–32 NIV1984

Years ago we were on a road trip with youth from our church and stopped at a truck stop to eat. When it came time to get everyone back on the bus, I saw that many of the young people were in a video arcade. As I walked in I noticed one particular pinball game that had the word *Revolution* emblazoned across the top. Just under that word was the statement, "The Music Is the Weapon."

The enemy has known for a long time that music is a weapon. In the 1960s, an entire cultural revolution was driven by a style of music. The Beatles wrote a song proclaiming what was happening and called it "Revolution." Today the Church is taking this weapon back and wielding it against our foe, causing God to arise. Let the high praises of God be in our mouths and a two-edged sword in our hands (see Psalm 149:6)!

The Weapon of Proclamations and Decrees

Job 22:28 gives us insight into the power of decrees: "You will also decree a thing, and it will be established for you; and light will shine on your ways" (NASB).

In the days of biblical kings, we read how their proclamations and decrees would instantly shift the law of the land and the atmosphere in which people lived. From the book of Esther we know that an evil decree of death and destruction was written against the Jewish people by the king's highest ranking noble, Haman. The decree gave the order to annihilate the Jews and take their property all in one single day (see Esther 3:13). That sounds just like the devil!

In desperation Esther went before the king. She found favor in his sight and told him of the plot against her people. The king responded with these words to Esther and her uncle Mordecai: "You yourselves write a decree concerning the Jews, as you please, in the king's name, and seal it with the king's signet ring; for whatever is written in the king's name and sealed with the king's signet ring no one can revoke" (Esther 8:8).

What decree did Esther and Mordecai write? They wrote a decree authorizing God's people to fight back. The decree stated that those enemies who assaulted the Jews would forfeit their own lives and property.

Today, God's "Esther" Church is arising and coming before His throne of grace. His scepter of favor has been extended to us, and He is saying to us, "You yourselves write a decree."

Regardless of what the devil has decreed against us, we have been empowered to overrule him. Our new decree makes the enemy's decree illegal and ineffective. The Church must flood the spiritual atmosphere with all that God is saying and decreeing in the earth. Because of Esther's decree, "on the day that the enemies of the Jews had hoped to overpower them, the opposite [reverse] occurred, in that the Jews themselves overpowered those who hated them" (Esther 9:1).

Several years ago God spoke to me from the above verse, and told me we had entered a time of "divine reversals." I knew that God was declaring this and that we in turn were to decree it. After extensive study and prayer I emerged from my office full of faith and excitement for what was to come.

Within hours, though, we had to lay hold of this word for a miracle for our young grandson who had been diagnosed with compression on his brain. Because of several other physical challenges doctors were hesitant to operate. They decided to postpone surgery until he was a bit older, but cautioned his parents that several bad things could happen as a result. One of the dangers stemmed from the location of the compression in his brain: He could lose the use of an arm or leg. If that occurred, the doctors explained, the damage would be irreversible.

That very day God spoke to me to have the Body of Christ decree a "divine reversal." My grandson was already beginning to lose the use of his left leg. He was dragging it behind him as he tried to walk and even when he crawled. The doctor told his parents that this was to be expected in this situation, and that the damage was irreversible.

The doctors said "irreversible," but God decreed "divine reversal"! We laid hands on our little grandson and decreed the Word of the Lord.

That day nothing improved. The second day, he got worse. But we continued to decree "divine reversal." On the third day he woke up, jumped out of bed and ran around the house—his leg completely restored.

The decree was our weapon to fight for our grandson's healing. Since that time we have seen many reversals: barrenness, blindness, deafness, diseases—all reversed! Prodigals have turned around and come back to God. Lawsuits have been miraculously settled in favor of believers. Debt has been forgiven. Homes in bankruptcy have been restored to permanent ownerships. Even cities and nations have experienced turnarounds as the people of God began to rise, pray and decree God's reversals. The decree is truly a weapon to overcome the enemy.

The Weapon of Prophecy

Isaiah 30:31 declares that the voice of the Lord will shatter the enemy. When God speaks, things change. Remember, a basic definition of *prophecy* is "hearing what God is saying and then speaking it out loud." When we say what God says, prophecy becomes a weapon of war to beat back the enemy. Paul charged Timothy, who was at this point overseeing the church in Ephesus in the midst of great persecution and trouble, to use the prophecies that had been spoken over him, "that by them you may wage the good warfare" (1 Timothy 1:18). Prophecy is a weapon!

In the familiar story found in Ezekiel 37, we read how God took the prophet Ezekiel to a valley filled with dry bones and asked him, "Can these bones live?"

Ezekiel answered, "Only You know, Lord."

That was not a very faith-filled statement in my opinion. But then God gave him instructions: "Prophesy to the dry bones!"

What were these dry bones? This was the site of a terrible battle where fallen soldiers were not buried honorably. It was a place of horrible defeat. The Hebrew word for *dry bones* comes from the convergence of three words: *shame, disappointment* and *confusion*. God was teaching the prophet that the way to break hopelessness and defeat is to prophesy to the places of

195

shame, disappointment and confusion. When we do, the dry bones come alive, fit together and stand up as an exceedingly great army.

I once prophesied over a young lady who seemed to have a defiant attitude toward receiving a word from God.

The Lord said to her, "You are not forgotten."

When this simple word was spoken she began to weep uncontrollably. She threw her arms around me and hugged me tightly. Then she rolled up her sleeve and showed me where she had taken a knife and carved the word *Forgotten* into her forearm.

God said she was *not* forgotten. The prophetic word became a weapon against all her shame, disappointment and confusion and allowed her to open her heart to the Lord. She has since given her testimony of His love and transforming power.

The Weapon of Peace

One of the first things the enemy wants to rob from believers is our peace. If the devil gets us out of peace into fear, doubt and unbelief, then our faith and discernment cannot operate effectively.

We must be vigilant to discern how the enemy is stealing our peace and get our minds and hearts focused once again upon the beauty, majesty and power of the Lord (see John 14:27; 16:33). Part of our warfare involves taking every thought captive and making it obedient to Christ (see 2 Corinthians 10:5). When we align ourselves with the Prince of Peace, He arises on our behalf to deal with all enemies.

This is where we find victory: "The God of peace will swiftly pound Satan to a pulp under your feet! And the wonderful favor of our Lord Jesus will surround you" (Romans 16:20 TPT).

The prophet Isaiah declared,

In that day this song will be sung in the land of Judah: "We have a strong city; God will appoint salvation for walls and bulwarks. Open the gates, that the righteous nation which keeps the truth may enter in. You will keep him in perfect peace, whose mind is stayed on You, because he trusts in You. Trust in the LORD forever, for in YAH, the LORD, is everlasting strength."

Isaiah 26:1–4

As we keep our hearts set on the Lord, God will keep us in peace and defend us.

The Weapon of Prosperity

God gives us power to create wealth, and wealth, when properly stewarded, brings influence. But how is that a weapon against darkness?

We read this in the book of Deuteronomy: "And you shall remember the LORD your God, for it is He who gives you power to get wealth, that He may establish His covenant which He swore to your fathers, as it is this day" (Deuteronomy 8:18). The word for *power* is the Hebrew word *koakh*, which means "force, might, strength and ability." Prosperity is a force. So is poverty. When Satan seeks to hold individuals or even territories in captivity, he will seek to control the resources. Satan actually controls people and regions by locking up wealth. It is what happened in our territory until God gave us discernment.

When the Kingdom of God prospers in a region, it causes an economic shift that will break the stranglehold of darkness. We see this in Acts 19 when Paul preached the Gospel in Ephesus for two years. The craftsmen of the city left him alone until sales dropped on their silver statues of Diana. The economy of the city shifted because the Kingdom of God was expanding. When the tradesmen realized this they began shouting against Paul until the whole city was in an uproar. Satan's hold on the city was shifting.

197

A dear friend and powerful prophet named Sharon Stone, who is the director of Christian International Europe, put this into action. One day as she was sitting at a traffic light in our area she noticed a palm reader's place of business and began to rebuke the spirit of witchcraft.

She heard the Lord speak and say, *Don't pray that way. Instead, pray that her source of income dries up so she goes out of business.*

So she prayed and decreed what God had said. Suddenly the front door of the business flew open, a woman with long flowing robes ran out, shook her fists at the sky and screamed, "No!"

Hmmm, Sharon thought. *We must be on to something here!* Within a matter of months the palm reader's business was shut down, though it had been there for at least a decade.

The Weapon of Prophetic Acts

Throughout Scripture the prophets of old demonstrated their messages through prophetic acts. Isaiah walked naked for three years as a sign and wonder against Egypt (see Isaiah 20:2–3). Ezekiel lay on his right side for 390 days then on his left side for forty days to demonstrate bearing the iniquities of the house of Israel and the house of Judah (see Ezekiel 4:4–8). These communicated God's messages to Israel. At other times prophetic acts released the power of God. We see this demonstrated as Moses cast down his rod before the throne of Pharaoh, and it became a serpent that swallowed up the serpents of the sorcerers. Or when Moses lifted the rod and parted the Red Sea. These demonstrations conducted the power of God into the earth realm.

As I mentioned earlier, Bishop Hamon loves to get people engaged in a prophetic act of warring against the enemy by shouting. He also leads us in motions of boxing as though punching the enemy. It is a prophetic act that declares defeat to the kingdom of darkness.

A few years ago he activated three thousand people in southern Nigeria to fight for their nation since radical Islamic forces were encroaching their borders. Boko Haram had crossed the northwestern border of southern Nigeria and ISIS was invading the northeastern border. The people of God punched and shouted and prayed in tongues for almost an hour and left with a sense of victory. Four days later the news sources announced that the radical Islamic forces had been pushed back in the west and the east and driven out of their territory. As the prophetic act was demonstrated, God sent angelic forces to empower the Nigerian armies to win the battle.

Daniel 11:32 declares this: "The people who know their God shall be strong, and carry out great exploits." Whenever we make a stand for the Lord, God will fight for us! As we employ our spiritual weapons of war we are empowered to push back the gates of hell and advance the Kingdom of God. Let us fight the good fight of faith. We will see territories transformed and people set free.

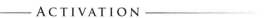

ACTIVATION

Think of an area where you desire breakthrough. Select one or more of the spiritual weapons listed above and begin to employ it against your enemy and for your victory.

12

DISCERNMENT AND INTERCESSION TO TRANSFORM TERRITORIES

Surely His salvation is near to those who fear Him,
that glory may dwell in our land.

Psalm 85:9

Every time Tom and I travel to a city or nation, we listen to discern both the voice of God for the region as well as the voice of the enemy against it. This helps local leaders have clearer insight and direction for their churches to align with God's decrees over the land and, at times, to rise up and do spiritual battle against an identified foe and false decrees.

On our first transatlantic ministry trip, Tom and I traveled to the Netherlands and held meetings the day we arrived. I was experiencing jet lag but I pressed on, keeping my spirit man alive and charged up by praying in tongues.

During a time of worship I had one of my first open visions. It was as though a curtain got pulled back, and I saw into the second heaven. I saw a map of the northern part of Europe and five demonic rulers standing in a circle over it.

One of the principalities noticed I could see them and proudly announced, "I am Ashkelon, prince of the Netherlands." Then suddenly the curtain closed. The whole vision only lasted two or three seconds. I had never heard of anything like this happening, but I sat down and wrote what I had seen.

Later I shared my vision with Tom, and we began to seek the Lord about the meaning. Here is what we discerned from this very brief vision.

Ashkelon was one of five chief Philistine cities. It was a major port city by which supplies came into the land from the sea. The name means "I will be weighed." The biblical example of this was when God brought Israel out of Egypt and told them to cross into the Promised Land. They "weighed" what God said against the giants in the land, and refused to go forward. For their disobedience, they wandered in the wilderness for forty years.

When we shared this vision with the leaders, noting that the Netherlands was the largest port nation in Europe and that God wanted to make them a land of spiritual resource, the leaders explained their history of rejecting any move of God. They told us that when the Welsh revival was in full swing, church fathers in the Netherlands sent six men to check out what God was doing, just as the twelve spies were sent to check out Canaan. When the men returned, all agreed that it was an amazing move of God, but five of the men had reservations about it. They feared that if they welcomed it into their nation it would disrupt their religious organization.

The sixth man, like Joshua and Caleb, said, "This is God! We need to embrace this move." But the leaders "weighed" what God had said and decided to decline, missing their hour of visitation.

The leaders told Tom and me other stories of times when church leaders had resisted a move of God. But this time, they cried out in repentance to the Lord and asked God to move in the nation again. They shouted and declared they would receive the move of God. They rebuked the Ashkelon assignment against them, in Jesus' name. Discernment turned into deliverance and alignment with the purposes of God. From that time forward, many leaders and churches in that nation aligned with the apostolic prophetic movement and embraced the fullness of the outpouring of the Holy Spirit.

If you recall, there were four other demonic powers in the vision. I believe they represented other nations of Europe in the grip of four other Philistine strongholds. In my opinion, this is how they correlate.

The name *Ekron* means "eradication, to be torn up by the roots, extermination." Ekron was a divided city and home to the temple for Beelzebub, thus a hub of idolatry and perversion. I believe this could be a demonic assignment against Belgium. This is a nation divided by language and a stronghold of humanism. A demonic assignment could be in operation against that land to eradicate Christianity from its borders.

The name *Ashdod* means "ravager, robber; powerful, impregnable; to oppress and destroy." Here was the center of military might of the Philistines where they worshiped Dagon, the fish god. Part of the worship involved getting drunk on a kind of alcohol made out of grain. I believe this could be a demonic assignment against Germany to ravage the land spiritually instead of allowing it to be the land of reformation God created it to be.

The name *Gath* means "winepress." This points to France, famous for its wine. Gath was home to the race of giants whom Joshua never fully defeated. They were not conquered until

David's reign. This could represent a stubborn foe that will be overthrown by a Davidic company.

The name *Gaza* means "the strong; mighty, greedy, powerful." The city was a commercial and military junction and the financial center of the Philistines. I believe this could represent an assignment against England to lock up righteous wealth through greed and power.

It is interesting how much information can come from a two- or three-second vision! This is just one example of how God reveals spiritual opposition over nations to the leaders of the land. Whether you are traveling and ministering to presidents, prophesying to nations, pastoring a local flock or on your knees in your prayer closet, God is looking for individuals with discernment who will understand the hidden things so that they can be revealed, breakthrough can come, and captives can be set free.

Discerning the *Ekklesia*

Jesus chose a specific term to describe what He had come to build in the earth. Look at His words: "I will build My church, and the gates of Hades shall not prevail against it" (Matthew 16:18). He did not say, "I will construct a building" or "I will gather a body of worshipers." He used a term of the day, one used by the secular government, to describe the Church He had come to build.

The word *church* is translated from the Greek word *ekklesia*, which means "the called-out ones." This term originated in Greece and referred to a ruling legislative body formed by calling out men who were over the age of eighteen and who had served two years of military service. This group, or assembly, formed the legislative body that ruled ancient Greek culture.

After conquering Greece, Rome continued using this term governmentally and legislatively; however, they also appropriated it militarily. The Roman military *ekklesia* were those called out of the regular military ranks to form a specialized task force. Their mission was to carry out the directives of the emperor/king ensuring that his will was implemented across the kingdom. Their job was to make all the newly conquered territory look like Rome: to establish culture that looked like Rome, to build roads and buildings that looked like Rome, to replicate and extend the rulership to look like Rome.

This is the structure Jesus had in mind when He taught His disciples to pray, "Let your kingdom come. Let your will be done on earth as it is done in heaven" (Matthew 6:10 GW). This phrase literally means "to superimpose heaven on earth." Our job as the *ekklesia* is to superimpose the rule of the Kingdom of heaven on the earth wherever we go. That means we need to confront illegitimate and illegal rulers in the spirit realm in order to advance a spiritual Kingdom.

Built on the Foundation of Apostles and Prophets

Ephesians 2:20 tells us the Church, or *ekklesia*, is "built on the foundation of apostles and prophets, Jesus Christ Himself being the chief cornerstone." In Tom's book *7 Anointings for Kingdom Transformation* (Christian International, 2016), he writes about apostles and prophets being vital to possess our land:

> So what does it mean to be "apostolic"? The term is taken from the Greek word "apostollos," which denotes one who is "a delegate, a messenger, one sent forth with orders, one sent on a mission." As the people of God, we are sent on a mission into this earth, as delegates or ambassadors of God's Kingdom to establish Kingdom rule everywhere we go. . . . In order for us to advance, we have to be constantly looking ahead. That means because the apostolic and prophetic are not only foundational but revelational ministries, they bring something essential for the church to advance. . . . Apostles and prophets are looking

to raise up a pioneer Joshua Generation that is seeking God for ways to possess their land. They are not willing to just settle into a comfort zone but are always looking for the new that God wants to say and do. They confront the status quo and challenge the Church to move, shift, change, adapt and advance. They create a "we are well able" faith atmosphere that causes courage to confront the overpowering enemies and the established powers. They will not cower in the face of giants and walled cities that mock them. They recognize they were made to contend to take the land.

Scripture is clear that the Church needs apostles and prophets functioning in order for it to be properly founded, built and established. Ephesians 4:11–12 tells us that God gave apostles, prophets, evangelists, pastors and teachers to equip the saints for the work of ministry. Most churches are familiar with the functions of evangelists, pastors and teachers; however, God has recently restored the ministry functions of apostles and prophets to the Church as well. These ministries center around hearing the voice of God and moving in supernatural power to impact lives and even regions. Apostles and prophets challenge the Church to operate in the supernatural dimension and get God's heart, not just for people but for territories as well.

While not every believer is called to be an evangelist, all are called to win souls. Not every believer is a pastor or a teacher, but we are all called to represent the heart of Christ and make disciples. Similarly, not all are called to be prophets or apostles, but every believer is called to be prophetic and hear the voice of God, as well as apostolic, to be sent on Kingdom missions in the earth with signs and wonders accompanying them. It is truly only as apostolic and prophetic anointing is present that discernment operates to its fullest with the Spirit of wisdom and revelation.

Calling Watchmen and Intercessors

Within the *ekklesia* God is calling everyone who will engage in the necessary roles of watchman and intercessor. Both functions need clear spiritual discernment to be most effective. Jesus calls us to watch and pray (see Matthew 26:41; Mark 13:33). Intercessors are those who carry the call and anointing of Issachar, those who are willing to bear God's burdens in prayer to see God's plans implemented in the earth.

J. Hudson Taylor, nineteenth-century British missionary and founder of China Inland Mission, said this:

> The power of prayer has never been tried to its full capacity in any church. If we want to see mighty wonders of divine grace and power wrought in the place of weakness, failure and disappointment, let the whole Church answer God's standing challenge: "Call unto me, and I will answer thee, and show thee great and mighty things, which thou knowest not."*

His prayer life enabled him to penetrate a hostile nation with the Gospel. At the end of his life there were more than 800 missionaries and more than 125,000 Christians in China. He is known as the father of modern missions. Every believer is called to be an intercessor.

Along with the call to pray, God is anointing us to watch. The prophet Isaiah gives us this picture: "On your walls, O Jerusalem, I have appointed watchmen; all day and all night they will never keep silent. You who remind the LORD, take no rest for yourselves" (Isaiah 62:6). In the Old Testament watchmen were guards out on the hilltops keeping an eye on the harvests and also sentinels on the walls of the city looking into the distance in order to announce that someone was approaching.

*Sermon Index, "Powerful Quotes on Prayer," http://www.sermonindex.net/modules/newbb/viewtopic.php?topic_id=36715&forum=34.

This is a prophetic positioning that involves seeing, discerning and protecting.

The three words translated *watchman* in Hebrew are *natsar*, "to protect, observe, preserve and see hidden things"; *shamar*, "to keep, guard, protect, preserve"; and *tsaphah*, "to lean forward and peer into the distance, to keep watch, spy." This tells us that the responsibility of the spiritual watchman is to lean forward and peer into the distance and see the hidden things in order to guard, protect and preserve. Ezekiel was a watchman for Israel and stated that part of his role was to watch over and preserve the holiness of the Lord in the land by identifying that which was unclean. God gave this directive to Ezekiel: "And they [the priests] shall teach My people the difference between the holy and the unholy, and cause them to discern between the unclean and the clean" (Ezekiel 44:23).

In his book *Watchman Prayer* (Bethany, 2008) Dutch Sheets says the watchmen were positioned to see both messengers and enemies as they approached the city and would sound the alarm as necessary. Dutch writes further: "Watchmen do this today in a spiritual sense. They alert the Body of Christ to attacks of the enemy, sounding the alarm. When the watchmen are functioning properly, we need never be caught off guard by Satan and his forces."

As we use the gift of discernment we must couple revelation with deeper authority in our prayer lives. Watching must be accompanied by praying. Praying must be accompanied by watching. Paul tells us to be "praying always with all prayer and supplication in the Spirit, being watchful" (Ephesians 6:18). Peter gives us a powerful image in this regard. We must always be vigilant because "our adversary, the devil, as a roaring lion, walks about seeking whom he may devour" (1 Peter 5:8). The Greek word for *vigilant* means "to watch, to stay awake, to pay close attention to." Watching and praying are vital for waging successful spiritual warfare, as they involve contending with the adversary.

We must learn to pray the Word, for God's Word does not return void (see Isaiah 55:11). We must learn to keep a journal or a record of what we are seeing and hearing so we can watch with God over His Word to see Him perform it (see Jeremiah 1:12). We must be willing to study to show ourselves approved to God (see 2 Timothy 2:15). We must learn to prophesy and decree what we discern (see Job 22:28). As we learn to pray with other skilled intercessors and begin to merge that which we discern with their revelations, we will be in a better position to receive the full picture of all God is doing.

There is a new prayer movement arising with apostles, prophets, watchmen and intercessors functioning in unity, synergizing wisdom, revelation and discernment to bring transformation. There is an awakening within the Body of Christ for each one to do his or her part. Cities and nations are hanging in the balance in this critical hour.

How Nations Change

God said to the prophet Jeremiah, "See, I have this day set you over the nations and over the kingdoms, to root out and to pull down, to destroy and to throw down, to build and to plant" (Jeremiah 1:10). God anointed the Persian king Cyrus for a specific mission and took hold of his hand to help him subdue nations (see Isaiah 45:1). The early Church transformed cities and regions through the power of the Gospel of the Kingdom and the demonstration of the Holy Spirit. They were known as those "who have turned the world upside down" (Acts 17:6).

I believe God gives certain people assignments over nations. Prophets, apostles, governmental leaders, business leaders may have greater positioning to exercise spiritual authority to implement change on a large scale, but all believers are authorized to utilize spiritual authority in their personal spheres of influence.

Below are five steps that you can apply to any battle you find yourself called to—whether it is the corrupt politics of a nation or an unbiblical program in your local elementary school.

But let me add a word of caution: God always has a time, a strategy and a people who are called to bring change. Discernment is more than seeing a demonic stronghold or a corrupt system in the earth; it is also discerning your personal role in exposing and dismantling those structures. Some may feel called to pray; others may feel called to run for office or take positions of influence within the territory. If you feel you are to be part of the intercessory force to bring freedom, find the people you are to pray with, for you must not try to deal with a territorial stronghold alone. Together with your team discern God's strategy, both short term and long term, for praying in a change, as well as any natural assignments of involvement God may have you engage in. Finally, remember that God always has specific timing in dealing with unrighteous structures and strongholds. Those who are mature will be patient to allow God to reveal both time and strategy for maximum Kingdom impact.

When speaking of changing the structure of a nation we can learn a lot from a modern war scenario. Here are strategies that have been used successfully to conquer oppressive spiritual regimes.

Awakening

One of the first steps is to recognize the need for change in order for justice to be done and people to be liberated. Believers can become acclimatized to corruption and darkness in their land and may find themselves blind to the actual need for change. Awakening must first occur so that mobilization can take place. The Church must be awakened to her identity as the

210

ekklesia, the rulers and legislators in the earth, His Kingdom representatives to bring change.

The War Council

Next, leaders form a war council where strategies and plans are made to bring liberation. In high-level warfare this is when apostles, prophets and other spiritual leaders release the strategy God has given them. This is the focus believers need for the assignment ahead. It is the spiritual leaders' responsibility to steward the word that has been spoken over a nation. Apostolic and prophetic councils discern the strategy God is providing for both intercession and the dissemination of the word.

The Air War

Modern times have shown us a successful pattern of warfare. First send in an air force to establish "air superiority." Once the fly zones are secured it makes it much easier for the boots on the ground, which will actually implement a governmental shift. Spiritually speaking, the air initiative that strikes to change the spiritual atmosphere over a nation is implemented through focused prayer, prophetic words, decrees and worship.

Part of the air war might include control of the airwaves (media, news, entertainment). The enemy always seeks to control the narrative given over the airwaves, through propaganda and a bombardment of ideologies, in order to demoralize the troops. This part of the prayer assignment includes an invasion of key voices and righteous narratives into the communication channels in order to lessen the enemy's control.

The Ground War

This is when soldiers actually go into the land and begin to overthrow a government, subdue the enemy and set people free. We see this as a spiritual pattern in the book of Acts:

Then Philip went down to the city of Samaria and preached Christ to them. And the multitudes with one accord heeded the things spoken by Philip, hearing and seeing the miracles which he did. For unclean spirits, crying with a loud voice, came out of many who were possessed; and many who were paralyzed and lame were healed. And there was great joy in that city.

Acts 8:5–8

Without boots on the ground, there can be no territorial shift or possessing the land. This may mean we walk the land doing prophetic acts such as pouring oil or making decrees. Or this may mean we come out of our prayer closets and, like Philip, impact the lives of the people living in the land with demonstrations of the power of God. We overthrow the oppression of the previous spiritual dictator who has kept the people and the city in captivity. When you deliver your neighbor's son from a spirit of addiction, there will be great joy in your city. When you release healing to your coworker who is dying of cancer, you will bring great joy to your city. When we do the works of Christ, the people of the land will realize the Kingdom of heaven has come to them.

New Governance

After the enemy is subdued a new government must be established that reflects the values of the winners of the conflict. For believers, what begins in prayer, prophecy and proclamations must be followed up by seeing that the righteous are placed in positions of influence to promote the righteous change. This would involve having key leaders/Kingdom influencers in education, government and the business realms as well as every sector of society to bring a Kingdom mindset.

This is discipling of nations.

Discernment Principles for Territorial Transformation

Discernment is vital when engaging in territorial transformation. When watching and discerning in the Spirit, we may be looking for more than just the identity of the strong man. In order to expose and deal with principalities and powers we may also need to recognize some of his more subtle tactics that hold his power in place. Here are some of the things you could be empowered to see.

Discernment Reveals Demonic Plans

Several years ago I was preaching at a large, open-air crusade in Managua, Nicaragua. In the middle of preaching I began to prophesy about an organized gathering of witches who were fasting and praying to invoke a natural disaster in the nation. Their purpose, I prophesied, was to destabilize the nation so their evil agenda could be advanced.

The people began to shout with a mighty roar. It was then explained to me that the current president's wife, Rosario Murillo, was a witch and that she had called for a national convening of witches to fast and pray for control of their nation. This was known by the churches there, but not by me! God revealed it so we could pray corporately and turn back the witchcraft sent to destroy the nation.

It was interesting that a few days later a late-season hurricane developed off the coast of Nicaragua, which is very unusual. Forecasters were predicting devastation from flooding and mudslides. But the enemy's plan had been revealed. The hurricane did not come ashore. It stalled out over the ocean and abruptly changed direction. Discernment enabled us to confront occult powers and disrupt the demonic assignments.

Discernment Exposes Unrighteous Decrees

Discerning God's decree over a territory is crucial. Every nation has a redemptive gift and purpose that the enemy wants

213

to pervert and destroy. The kingdom of darkness will always try to implement the opposite of what God has determined. Scripture says, "Woe unto those who decree unrighteous decrees" (Isaiah 10:1).

Sometimes God's decree is brought to light by observing the negative impact of the enemy's plan and knowing that God has decreed the opposite. If you look, for example, at certain African or South American nations that struggle with poverty and governmental corruption, you can also see that God has blessed many of these nations with tremendous natural resources. God first declared prosperity, then the enemy declared the opposite, poverty.

At times you will find that a decree, either in the natural or in the spiritual, is laying claim to a city or territory; it must be reversed in order to lay claim for the Kingdom of God. When this is uncovered, it might be necessary to write a new decree to declare what God says in place of what the enemy has decreed (see Esther 8:8). Decrees must be spoken out loud with authority. It can also be important to write down your decrees so they can be easily repeated and recorded.

When our area in Florida was locked up by a spirit of poverty, we discovered in our county record books, dating to the early 1900s, that our land was referred to as "Poor Man's Island." We wrote a new decree, declaring that we were a land of blessing and prosperity. When ministering in Glasgow, Scotland, with our friends Emma and David Stark, Tom and I were speaking in the oldest cathedral in Scotland. This was one of the last places where healing miracles were recorded before the Church went into the dark ages. During our ministry there we learned that Glasgow had a nickname: "The Sick Man of Europe." We wrote and declared a new decree over that city, believing that God would once again visit them with signs, wonders and miracles.

Discernment Exposes Detrimental Mindsets

At times God's prophetic word to a territory has difficulty breaking through because the people of the land are being controlled by an ungodly mindset. In that case, it is necessary to discern the existence of the mental stronghold in order to see God's word take root and give people the opportunity to repent and be free of the ungodly limitations.

Tom and I minister in Norway on a regular basis. On one occasion I knew that the Lord wanted to release His decree that Norway be a land and people of favor. I explained that this meant God would do special things for them. God would bless them as He did Abraham of old. He would make their names great, and they would be blessed to be a blessing (see Genesis 12:1–3).

God wanted to break limitation off the minds of the people, so I asked them to repeat this positive decree: "I am blessed and highly favored. God will bless me so I can be a blessing." It was an uplifting, hopeful word, but the people had a hard time repeating it. I realized I was hitting something in the spirit realm that was blocking their minds from receiving the word.

It was not hard to discover the problem. There is a national mindset from a code of conduct that was meant to promote equality in the Nordic culture, and that is referred to as the Law of Jante. While these might sound at first like humble and noble thoughts, they initiated a mindset of personal dejection and death of ambition that was preventing the people from grasping the spiritual concept of favor.

The ten rules of Jante Law state:

You're not to think you are anything special.

You're not to think you are as good as us.

You're not to think you are smarter than us.

You're not to convince yourself that you are better than us.

You're not to think you know more than us.

You're not to think you are more important than us.

You're not to think you are good at anything.

You're not to laugh at us.

You're not to think anyone cares about you.

You're not to think you can teach us anything.

As this was uncovered, the people of God had the opportunity to properly align to the Word of God and to repent of any limitation they had unintentionally set against God's blessing them.

Discernment Exposes Corruption

Quite often God will use prophets, watchmen and intercessors to discern and pray about hidden corruption occurring in a territory so that righteousness and truth can prevail. Sometimes there must be a rooting up, tearing down, throwing down and destroying what is in place in order for God and His Church to build and plant (see Jeremiah 1:10).

While speaking at a regional gathering in a neighboring county in Florida, Tom began to prophesy. He said, "The Lord says the good old boys in this county haven't been so good. He is getting ready to bring the things they have been doing in secret into the open. He will deal with the spirit of robbery in the county." The spiritual leaders began to pray about this issue and within months the sheriff and several others were arrested and sentenced to prison for crimes involving the theft and misappropriation of taxpayers' money.

On another occasion I traveled to Guatemala. I had a dream in which I saw the authorities breaking up a major sex-trafficking ring there. Later, when we gathered, I prophesied to that effect and had everyone join together to pray for God's justice to be released. Within a week headlines in the paper announced many arrests of ringleaders and many victims rescued.

At times the voice of God informs prophetically what is about to happen. At other times, a prophecy can set a chain of events in motion. Prophesied discernment leads to breakthrough!

Wisdom Strategies for Discernment

Paul wrote to the church at Ephesus, which was a city known as the center of magic and occult training. He prayed that God would grant them "the spirit of wisdom and revelation in the knowledge of Him" that the eyes of their understanding would be "enlightened" (Ephesians 1:17–18). The word *enlightened* is the Greek word *photizo* and means "to cause something to come to light and be clear to all." Paul knew that in order for the church in the city to thrive they would need to have the ability to bring things into the light and would need to operate in both wisdom and revelation. The following are some basic principles to help you when operating in discernment for your city, nation or region.

God Will Give Clear Strategy

Paul and Silas were on a missionary journey when the Holy Spirit seemingly blocked their way in order to get them in the right place at the right time:

> Now when they had gone through Phrygia and the region of Galatia, they were forbidden by the Holy Spirit to preach the word in Asia. After they had come to Mysia, they tried to go into Bithynia, but the Spirit did not permit them. So passing by Mysia, they came down to Troas. And a vision appeared to Paul in the night. A man of Macedonia stood and pleaded with him, saying, "Come over to Macedonia and help us." Now after he had seen the vision, immediately we sought to go to Macedonia, concluding that the Lord had called us to preach the gospel to them.
>
> Acts 16:6–10

217

According to the revelation from this dream, they went to Philippi, the chief city of Macedonia.

While there they led Lydia, a seller of purple, to the Lord. She and her whole household were baptized, which became the foundation of the church of the Philippians. Paul and Silas suffered for their obedience. They were beaten, thrown into prison and brought before the magistrates. God ultimately delivered them supernaturally from prison—and the jailor and all his household were also saved.

These men of faith discerned the plans and purposes of God, the strategy, regarding their assignment in the region, and a thriving church was birthed.

There Is Proper Timing Regarding What You Discern

Part of the strategy in dealing with what you discern must include timing: "A wise man's heart discerns both time and judgment, because for every matter there is a time and judgment" (Ecclesiastes 8:5–6).

Paul and Silas were arrested in Philippi for casting a spirit of divination out of a slave girl. She had been following them around the city for many days, crying out and saying, "These men are the servants of the Most High God, who proclaim to us the way of salvation" (Acts 16:17).

Though her statement was true, Paul discerned that it had a demonic root and was sent to disrupt the preaching of the Gospel. He put up with her for several days, no doubt realizing there could be a consequence to casting the devil out of her and not wanting to have his ministry time cut short.

But finally, "Paul, greatly annoyed, turned and said to the spirit, 'I command you in the name of Jesus Christ to come out of her.' And he came out that very hour" (verse 18).

Shortly after this, he and Silas were arrested, and his time of ministry in the city began to draw to a close. God always has a particular timing for dealing with what He shows you. Just because you discern something does not mean it is automatically time to deal with the situation. Rather, you must be sensitive to the process God has in place.

Never Deal with Territorial Strongholds Alone

In spiritual matters there is always strength in numbers. Leviticus 26:8 encourages us in this reality: "Five of you shall chase a hundred, and a hundred of you shall put ten thousand to flight." When we join our faith with that of other believers we present a synergized force the enemy cannot withstand. Remember, just because you discern something does not mean you deal with it all by yourself. In my experience I have found that it is actually dangerous for individual intercessors or watchmen to try to wage territorial spiritual warfare all by themselves. Stay connected to spiritual leaders and other intercessors. Know where you are called and whom you are called to serve with. Understand that the enemy's plan will try to separate and isolate you from others. Unity is always key to seeing sustainable victory in a region.

God is raising up a powerful *ekklesia* today, called to pray prayers, preach the Word of God and demonstrate God's Kingdom through signs and wonders that change nations. Discernment is key to tearing down strongholds and opening the gates for the King of glory. As we rise up and engage in the battle we will once again be known in the earth as "those who turn the world upside down."

─────────── A C T I V A T I O N ───────────

Think about the land where you live—your city, your state or your nation. What are some of the strongholds you see operating in your land? Discern what the enemy has decreed over your territory as a statement of his rule. Now discern what God first spoke over your territory. (Hint: It will be the opposite of what the enemy has decreed.) Write down what God decrees over your land and speak it out. Share this with your fellow intercessors to discern any prayer strategies for uprooting the enemy's false decree.

13

DISCERNING AND IDENTIFYING STRONGHOLDS

For the weapons of our warfare are not carnal, but
mighty through God to the pulling down of strong
holds.

2 Corinthians 10:4 KJV

One of the first times I traveled to Nashville, Tennessee,
for a prophetic conference, I had an encounter with a
demonic principality over the city. My plane was landing and
I was waking up from a nap, when suddenly two fierce spirits
confronted me and said the city belonged to them. I knew one
was a Jezebel spirit and the other was a Python spirit that had
wrapped itself around the city.

I have a prayer team that prays and discerns with me whenever I travel to minister. When I landed, I was a bit shaken by

the intensity of this encounter, so I opened my email to see what my team was sensing. My daughter and several other intercessors all commented that they sensed a strong Jezebel and Python spirit over Nashville, and that God would show me the seat of their power so that prayer could arise from the church and strongholds could be unseated.

As I went to my room, I began to walk the floor and pray. Why are these spirits entrenched in this city known for country music? It just did not make any sense. As I walked and prayed I picked up a magazine that advertised things to do locally. I was flipping through the pages, praying in the Spirit, when I saw a picture of a replica of the Parthenon of Athens. It is located west of the downtown area of Nashville. Inside the building is a 42-foot statue of Athena (a Jezebel type) covered in gold leaf with a thigh-high python snake at her side!

Well, well! This was obviously what God was showing me was affecting the city.

This parthenon is a full-scale replica of the Parthenon on the Acropolis of Athens, Greece. I learned that Nashville's nickname is "Athens of the South." The Parthenon in Athens was the temple of the virgin goddess Athena, who was considered to be the Greek goddess of wisdom, strategic warfare, the arts, crafts and skill. Nashville is a city dedicated to the arts, so this began to make some sense. The Tennessee Titans, a professional football team based in Nashville, offers another reference to Greek mythology. I realized I was going to need to study how this goddess spirit operates and the significance of the accompanying python in order to know how to direct our prayers effectively.

God's Purpose for Cities

Whenever we see a demonic stronghold try to take control of a city, region or nation it is important to understand what God originally determined would be the inheritance of that land. God is the Creator and the originator of every purpose under heaven: "The earth is the LORD's, and the fulness thereof; the world, and they that dwell therein" (Psalm 24:1 KJV). This earth does not belong to the devil or any of his minions; the earth belongs to the Lord. But the devil is a usurper and a counterfeiter and loves to take what God has decreed and try to decree the opposite. If God has decreed a territory to be prosperous, the enemy loves to declare poverty or loves to lock up the wealth of the land through greed and avarice. If a land is called to demonstrate God's justice, the enemy loves to fill it with injustice.

In the case of Nashville, the enemy encouraged the building of a false temple because the city was called to demonstrate true worship and be a prophetic center in the nation. Instead of honor for the goddess of arts, God's purpose was for Nashville to be a city that brings glory to the Most High God. It is called Music City for a reason and is also known as the Christian Music Capital of the World.

Building Strongholds for God

Part of our mission is to tear down the strongholds of the enemy. The word *stronghold* means "a well-fortified place or fortress." It also means "a place where a particular cause or belief is strongly upheld and guarded." These are places, either in our own minds or in territories, where the enemy has managed to entrench and fortify his kingdom of lies and establish a place of dominion. Fortresses were places to gather against attack but were also places where weapons and wealth were stored. Where you find a stronghold of the enemy, you normally also find a locking up of all kinds of resources.

But throughout history one finds an interesting principle about overthrowing strongholds. When a fortress was captured, the invading force generally did not tear it down. No, it was a valuable fortification that only needed to be reinforced so as to make it stronger, now for their use. The conquering army would build an even greater stronghold on the very spot. If they did not occupy the conquered fortress, their enemy would come back and attempt to reclaim what had been theirs.

We see this in the book of Judges. Judah fought against Kirjath Arba, the city of giants, and overthrew Sheshai, Ahiman and Talmai. This is the very spot where Judah established the famed city of Hebron, where David was anointed king over Judah and then all of Israel. They built a stronghold for God on top of the place their enemy once had a stronghold (see Judges 1:9).

This is exactly what God is calling His Church to do today. We are to overthrow darkness, and rebuild and fortify our land for God to move and reign in the earth. We are building a stronghold for the cause of Christ upon the very places the strongholds of the enemy have been established. Can we believe that college campuses, which have long been a stronghold for rebellion, lawlessness and the antichrist spirit, can be overtaken with revival and reformation and become a place where the glory of God is seen and proclaimed? Can we believe some of the darkest, most impoverished places on earth that suffer cruel injustice can become beacons of light? Can we see the kingdoms of this world become the kingdoms of our Lord and of His Christ (see Revelation 11:15)? I believe we can, and I believe we will!

What's in a Name?

I do not believe that we must have the particular name of a demonic spirit in order to pray effectively or wage spiritual warfare against it. There may be times, however, when God identifies a specific name or characteristic of a spirit in order for us to be the most strategic with our prayers, decrees and prophecies.

On one occasion in the early years of our church and ministry, it was apparent we were under some sort of spiritual attack. Our financial resources were drying up, many people were suffering from unusual sicknesses, and there seemed to be a great deal of confusion among our staff and leaders. Fortunately, we recognized we were not battling flesh and blood but that something was assigned to destroy us.

As I prayed I heard the Lord say that we were dealing with a spirit called Rahabar. I had no idea what that meant so I began to do some research about it.

I relayed a similar story in my introduction to this book regarding a spirit whose name was Tokamene. God helped me understand what the name meant as I looked it up phonetically in a Hebrew concordance. I did much the same with this new word—*Rahabar*. I found that Rahab is spoken of in Isaiah 51:9 and was also a poetic reference to Egypt: "Awake, awake, put on strength, O arm of the LORD! Awake as in the ancient days, in the generations of old. Are You not the arm that cut Rahab apart, and wounded the serpent?"

Rahab was believed to be a sea monster that guarded the Red Sea—the god of darkness, chaos and destruction—whom God cut apart when Israel miraculously crossed over on dry land. In Hebraic culture the word *bar* is used to indicate a son or someone in a particular linage (Simon bar Jonah—Simon the son of Jonah). What we were dealing with was a son of Rahab or god of chaos. That was it! We were dealing with a spirit of chaos and destruction that was standing in our path. We fasted, prayed and began spiritual warfare through worship and decrees. The Lord broke the power of this spirit off our ministry.

On a different occasion I had a dream in which I saw a demonic assignment coming against anointed apostolic and prophetic leaders. I knew the ringleader was someone called Rabshakeh. When I woke up I wondered if Rabshakeh was the name of a reggae band or what in the world that was supposed to mean.

When I went to the Scriptures I found that Isaiah 36–37 tells the story of the besiegement of Jerusalem by Sennacherib, king of Assyria. Hezekiah was king at the time and was a righteous reformer. Rabshakeh was the spokesman for Sennacherib, the mouthpiece of the enemy. He was sent to bring accusations against God and the king, and to tell the people how impossible their situation was. Rabshakeh was the voice of the devil trying to get into the hearts and minds of believers to get them to give up their fight. Never let the devil and his lies get into your head! I also believe this is a spirit that seeks to control the spiritual atmosphere by controlling the airwaves through the media and their antichrist agenda.

Understanding the name gave us a focus for watching and praying, exposing the tactics of the enemy and gaining victory in our battle.

Characteristics of Spiritual Strongholds

When identifying certain spiritual strongholds, such as Jezebel and Python, you can see that having a basic understanding from the Word of God about what these terms mean gives us an advantage. This section will give a brief description of the biblical context of several terms as well as identify characteristics of the operation of these spiritual forces. Many times studying the Old Testament names of Israel's enemies helps us understand some of the forces we deal with in our New Covenant warfare. Keep in mind that these are terms generally identified in intercession groups, but this is by no means an exhaustive list of strongholds to be contended with.

Here are meanings of some of the "ite" nations Israel faced and some of the demonic spirits we may discern in operation today (see Exodus 17:8; 34:11; Deuteronomy 7:1–7; 1 Samuel 14:48):

- *Amalekites.* This was the first enemy faced by Israel as an army coming out of Egypt. The name means "blood-licker." They were a tribe of raiders and plunderers of unsuspecting travelers and can be characterized as a spirit of robbery.

- *Canaanites.* The name means merchant but comes from a root word meaning "to bend the knee, to humiliate, to vanquish and bring low, to subdue, to humble" and represents a spirit of humiliation and shame.

- *Amorites.* This comes from a word meaning "one who makes announcements; lofty, prominent." It represents a spirit of pride and arrogance and a false prophetic spirit.

- *Perizzites.* This comes from a root word that means "to separate." It indicates a spirit of division.

- *Jebusites.* This comes from a root word that means "to be trodden down, desecrated or polluted." It represents an unclean spirit and compromise.

- *Hittites.* This comes from a word that means "terror." It represents a spirit of fear and intimidation.

- *Hivites.* In Joshua 9 we read that the Hivites deceived Israel into making a covenant of peace with them when Israel was commanded by God to destroy them. This tribe could represent a spirit of deception.

- *Girgashites.* This comes from a word that means "dwelling on clay soil." It represents a place where it is difficult for anything to grow. This could represent dealing with a spirit of oppression and suppression.

Let's now take a more in-depth look at various other names and characteristics of spiritual strongholds that seem to be commonly present when believers engage in spiritual warfare.

The Jezebel Spirit

Jezebel is the name given to two evil women in the Bible. The name holds the connotation of being "unchaste, unexalted and without cohabitation." In other words, no one can live with her. The first Jezebel in Scripture was the wife of King Ahab. She was from Zidon and was the daughter of Ethbaal, who was a priest of Baal and Ashtoreth. She moved to Jezreel and converted the city to Baal and Ashtoreth worship with all the idolatry and witchcraft she promoted. She supported 450 prophets of Baal and 400 prophets of Ashtoreth and had most of the true prophets of God killed, except, of course, for Elijah, who confronted her (see 1 Kings 16:30–33; 19:2; 2 Kings 9:22).

The second woman named Jezebel found in Scripture was in Thyatira (see Revelation 2:18–28). She was operating in the church, calling herself a prophetess yet leading people astray by her teachings—including seducing people into sexual immorality and into eating food sacrificed to idols (thereby partaking of idolatry). She was supposedly teaching her disciples the deep secrets of Satan.

The fact that the leaders were tolerating her and not dealing with her was a grave mistake, for God was getting ready to deal severely with her. But to those who overcame, God would give authority over nations.

The Jezebel spirit operates through a spirit of witchcraft, either outside the Church through idolatry, occult works and hidden practices or within the Church through seduction, manipulation, ungodly control, soulish prayers, confusion and intimidation. She will usurp authority over the appointed leader as she did with Ahab. Her goals are to stop the words of true prophets and promote that which is false. She hates women, especially prophetic women. She will attempt to rob believers of our spiritual inheritance, and will hire false accusers to destroy us, just as she did with Naboth. She operates through deception, sexual immorality, hopelessness and enticement to sin by doing that which is forbidden. She will use fear and intimidation—remember that Elijah wound up hiding in a cave—and attempt to get us to forfeit our spiritual assignments. She operates with a religious spirit with a goal of presenting something false and idolatrous rather than allow revival or reformation to come (see 1 Kings 18–21).

There are several things we need to understand about this spirit in order to deal with it properly. First, this is not a spirit that operates only through women; it is a demonic spirit that affects men and women alike. Laban, for example, controlled and manipulated Jacob for fourteen years; Saul controlled and intimidated David. Two examples of women that this spirit used to achieve her goals were Delilah, who used sexual seduction to manipulate Samson, and Herodias's daughter, who used her sexual powers to entice Herod into granting her request for the head of John the Baptist. I refer to this spirit with feminine pronouns because she is personified as a woman in Scripture. But make no mistake: This spirit works through male and female alike.

Secondly, this is not an identity given to humans. As I mentioned earlier, therefore, we should refrain from calling someone "a Jezebel." A person might be operating under the influence of a Jezebel spirit, but that person is not Jezebel. Jezebel is a spirit and must be treated accordingly. It is best to keep the person separated from the demonic spirit in your mind and conversation.

Thirdly, strong women are not Jezebels. Deborah was a strong woman leader, a judge and a prophetess. Esther was a righteous queen who saved a nation. These were strong women who were not operating under the influence of a demonic spirit. God is raising up strong women leaders today—Deborahs and Esthers who will change nations. Be careful if this is outside the paradigm of what you believe God is doing. Never assume that strong women leaders are operating through an illegitimate spirit.

One last point to make about the operation of this spirit comes from a vision I had during that prophetic conference in Nashville. As I was in a deep place of worship with the Lord, I was suddenly confronted by an ugly spirit that looked like Ursula, the Sea Witch from the Little Mermaid story. I knew this was the Jezebel spirit that God had warned me about, but I was not sure why I was seeing her in this form.

Then I remembered the story of the Little Mermaid: The Sea Witch stole the Little Mermaid's voice. I realized that one of the ways this spirit operates is to steal the voices of believers by physically attacking the mouth, vocal chords or breath. The other way is to steal the prophetic voice of influence from the mouths of believers.

As I alerted the people at the conference regarding what I had seen I found that at that conference, as well as other places where I have discerned Jezebel's operation, from sixty to eighty percent of the people present were affected physically regarding their voices, including many in the worship team, the prophets, leaders and intercessors. The remaining people present were being affected as well by Jezebel trying to cut off their prophetic voice of influence. As we prayed and broke the Jezebel assignment many people received immediate healing in their vocal chords, mouths and ability to breathe clearly.

Do not allow Jezebel to drive you into a cave of intimidation or shut down your prophetic voice. If you work with godly leaders and stir up your prophetic gifts, you may find yourself in a battle with this dark spirit of witchcraft. Do not be afraid. God has already won the victory over her, and she is already judged. It is time for you to execute the judgment written against her.

If you find yourself manifesting any of the characteristics of Jezebel through unrighteous control, manipulation, soulish prayers, seduction or intimidating others to do what you want, it is simple to break this spirit's power. Simply repent. Revelation 2:21 says that God gives us space to repent, or to turn away from ungodly behavior, even that which is demonically motivated. You always have a choice. The best way to deal with this spirit is to follow James 4:7, which says, "Therefore submit to God. Resist the devil and he will flee from you." At times submitting may mean putting yourself under the oversight of godly leaders and allowing them to speak into your life. This provides spiritual covering, safety, protection as well as freedom to rise to your potential without fear. Rise up and cast down the Jezebel spirit coming against you, and you will find boldness, courage and faith to overcome!

The Queen of Heaven

The Queen of Heaven is mentioned in Jeremiah as a false goddess worshiped by Israel during times they indulged in idolatry. Her followers reported that she did miracles, provided food and protected them when they worshiped her, but visited poverty and lack upon those who broke covenant with her (see Jeremiah 7:18–20; 44:15–19).

The Queen of Heaven refers to a goddess system of worship that was common in the ancient world. She was known as Ashtoreth in Canaan, as Astarte in the Middle East, as Ishtar in Babylon, as Aphrodite in Greece, as Venus in Rome, and as Diana or Artemis in Ephesus. Just about every polytheistic culture on earth worships a male god that controls harvest, grain, wealth and is often known as the sun god. Most of these male gods have a goddess who controls fertility, idolatry and family well-being who is most often known as a moon goddess.

Jezebel came from Zidon, which not only honored Baal and Ashtoreth but also worshiped the Queen of Heaven. As the wife of Ahab she became the evil personification of this ruling spirit, as did her daughter, Athaliah, who promoted building altars throughout the land to honor Baal and Ashtoreth.

Athaliah's name means "whom Jehovah afflicts or constrains" and comes from a root word meaning "to compress." The word *afflict* means "to distress with mental or bodily pain, to trouble greatly, to overthrow or defeat." The word *constrain* means "to confine forcibly, as by bonds, to repress." This evil manifestation of the Queen of Heaven spirit wants to afflict us and put us into bondage through physical or emotional pain, oppression, depression and hopelessness for the future.

This was one evil queen! When her son, King Ahaziah, was killed in battle she usurped the throne and killed her own grandchildren in order to keep it. This demonic assignment wants to cut off generational continuity and generational blessings. It wants to come after our children and children's children to afflict and constrain them in their walks with God.

But, fortunately, Athaliah missed the infant Joash, who was hidden away with his nurse for six years. After enduring six years of the destructive reign of Athaliah, the priest Jehoiada, whose name means "knowledge of God," sat seven-year-old Joash on the throne, proclaimed him to be the legitimate king, and gave orders for Athaliah to be killed. Then Jehoiada made a covenant between God, the new king and the people, that they would serve the Lord. The people overthrew the altars of Baal, bringing righteousness back to the land. Jehoiada was a reformer and a warrior. He fought for truth and righteousness and generational inheritance. Once Joash became king, his name was changed to Jehoash—from "given by the Lord" to "the fire of the Lord" (2 Kings 11).

The Serpent Spirits—Python and Leviathan

We noted earlier the story told in Acts 16 of Paul casting the spirit of divination out of a young slave girl "who brought her masters much profit by fortune-telling" (verse 16). The word *divination* in Greek is the word *puthon*, which indicates she was known as a pythoness. Python, in Greek mythology, was a god who guarded the Oracle of Delphi, the sanctuary where oracles, or false prophets, came to release their prophecies. We can see from this description that the python spirit is a spirit of divination or false prophecy that is rooted in occult practices and darkness.

In looking at the symbol of how this spirit presents itself, pythons are constricting snakes that choke the life out of their prey. They are ambush predators, who camouflage themselves and remain motionless, suddenly striking and wrapping themselves around their victims. When python is present you will find people who feel their life and energy being choked out as well as their hopes and dreams. They lose their ability to hear the voice of God and rather hear false prophecies of doom and gloom from the enemy. Python will use confusion, financial lack and fear to choke out your vision for the future. When watching the Disney movie *The Jungle Book*, I found it interesting that the python hypnotized and mesmerized the young boy in order to capture him. Beware of the hypnotizing effects of this spirit!

We live in the South in a rural area where we have to watch out for snakes. We know that snakes like to lie near doorways, probably to catch the heat from within the house. A Kenyan woman told me they make their children aware that often pythons will lie at the doorways of their homes, very still, awaiting an unsuspecting person to come through the door so it can spring into action and capture its prey.

This is interesting to me because Ezekiel 46:2 mentions that the prince came to "worship at the threshold" of the doorway. The Hebrew word for *threshold* is the word *miphtan*, which comes from a root word *pethen*, referring to "a twisting, contorting asp or python." So we see God's prince standing in the open door, worshiping God with his feet on the neck of his enemy! Whenever you are in a new season of God opening new doors, therefore, be aware that the enemy may have set a python on the threshold of your doorway to try to choke out the vision for your future and constrict resources and true revelation in your new day. But as you set your eyes to see and your heart to worship, you, too, can cause your feet to tread on serpents and scorpions.

Another serpent spirit, Leviathan, is called the king over the children of pride and is described as a many-headed monster who rules in the sea (see Job 41:34). The word *leviathan* means "a wreathed animal or serpent, especially the crocodile or some other sea monster; mourning." Job 41 paints a picture of a practically unconquerable foe. It describes a mighty creature, like a fire-breathing dragon, that seemingly cannot be stopped.

This spirit stirs up strife and contention through pride, arrogance, arguments and stubbornness. It stirs up criticism and causes people to become judgmental. It is independent and self-sufficient, resisting unity and unified efforts. It is one of the spirits behind prayerlessness and covenant breaking. It causes people to refuse to serve; instead, they align with a religious spirit. It hates the move of God and will resist change through fear and intimidation, resulting in apathy and hardened hearts in those it targets. Leviathan causes crooked, twisted communication and misunderstanding, which plays into his plan for division. One of the meanings of this name is "mourning." The enemy wants to cause mourning and grief through disappointment and injustice, thereby entrapping people into hopelessness. This can affect the life of an individual but quite often holds entire regions captive.

But God makes a different declaration: "In that day the LORD with his sore and great and strong sword shall punish leviathan the piercing serpent, even leviathan that crooked serpent; and he shall slay the dragon that is in the sea" (Isaiah 27:1 KJV). This spirit is described as a serpent. The Hebrew word *serpent* is the word *nachash*, which means "a hissing snake; to whisper a magic spell, to prognosticate, to enchant, to practice divination." This paints the picture of the dark occult nature of this spirit. Like python, this spirit will encourage witchcraft and divination to lead people away from the voice of God by twisting and distorting words.

But as fearsome as this spirit may seem, it is no match for the mighty hand of God. Scripture tells us that "[God] broke the heads of Leviathan in pieces, and gave him as food to the people inhabiting the wilderness" (Psalm 74:14). If you recognize the presence of this spirit, know that humility always answers pride, submission always answers independence, joy always answers grief, and a soft answer turns away wrath, division and strife.

Belial

The sons of Belial are mentioned throughout the Old Testament as troublemakers who brought accusation against the righteous. The word *Belial* comes from a Hebrew word meaning "worthlessness, wickedness, evil, naughtiness, ungodliness, ruin and destruction." It comes from a root word meaning "to cause you to fail by wearing you out." This is a spirit sent to harass you with trouble, to wear you down and wear you out until you quit. It is a spirit of weariness. It works in coordination with Jezebel to bring accusation against the righteous, as she did against Naboth (see 1 Kings 21:8–10). We read how this spirit drove men to commit horrible violent and perverse sexual acts (see Judges 19–20). It stirred strife and division between Israel and the tribe of Benjamin. The sons of Belial stood against David. This spirit will cause you to be divided from your leaders and from pressing in to prayer, worship and warfare. It also works with the spirit of robbery, as the sons of Eli acted like sons of Belial when they stole from the offering of the people given to the Lord (see 1 Samuel 2). The goal of this spirit is to rob you of your calling and destiny in Christ.

In her book *Seeing the Supernatural* (Chosen, 2017), Jennifer Eivaz writes:

> Belial is a spiritual power that works to make your life worthless and barren through idolatry and self-sabotaging behaviors. . . . Belial works to ensnare people into distinct sins so their lives are unfruitful and wasted. It partners with spiritual forces of wickedness to infect its territory with unrighteousness.

We must become aware of the works of this spirit and withstand its evil force.

The Absalom Spirit

Absalom was the third son of King David, and he ended up stealing the hearts of the men of Israel away from their anointed leader and usurping the throne. His name has come to represent a spirit of rebellion against appointed authority. This spirit is rooted in pride, ambition and unresolved offense, and will seek to destroy relationships within leadership teams or cause mistrust of one's leader. Angry that David did not properly defend or give justice to his abused sister, Tamar, Absalom rose up and took vengeance into his own hands. His pride left him with a wounded, critical spirit and a victim mentality that got him out of alignment with God's chosen leader. He rebelled, and it eventually cost him his life.

The Antichrist Spirit

First John 2:18 tells us that there are many antichrists. This term does not refer only to the man in the Tribulation who will deceive the world but is a term that indicates any person, system or theology that opposes Christ, His Gospel or His anointing: "Many deceivers have gone out into the world who do not confess Jesus Christ as coming in the flesh. This is a deceiver and an antichrist" (2 John 1:7).

The term *antichrist* comes from the combination of two Greek words: *anti* meaning "opposite or instead of, over against" and *christos* meaning "anointed one, the Messiah, Christ." Anything, therefore, that is against or opposite to Christ, the move of His Holy Spirit or His Church (since the word *Christian* means "anointed ones") is an antichrist. Antichrist brings a spirit of blindness against truth and leads people astray. It is the "god of this world" (2 Corinthians 4:4 NASB).

It is obvious that satanic cults, witchcraft covens and all manner of occult activities constitute an antichrist spirit. It can also be seen in abundance on college campuses where humanism, atheism, agnosticism and skepticism are all prevalent. We can also see antichrist in false religions, cults and any offshoot of Christianity that denigrates the deity of Christ or the fact of the physical resurrection of His body.

The above manifestations of antichrist in the earth are very concerning, especially as we witness the widespread effect on the younger generations and even on the structures of nations. I am equally concerned, however, with the manifestation of antichrist within the Church—those who are called to exemplify Jesus' light and life. I am concerned that people are not discerning the drift from biblical truth by many leaders today. I am concerned that people are not discerning the encroachment of universalism and polytheism into their churches, which promote the ideas that everyone will be saved, there is no penalty for sin, and there are many paths toward God. I am concerned that people are not discerning the imbalanced false grace message as well as the new generation of Judaizers who want to bring people back under ceremonial law. I am concerned that people are not discerning a false tolerance message spoken by those who decide that sin is not really sin because they are more compassionate than God. I am concerned that people are not discerning prejudice in the Church over race and gender—there is even a rise of anti-Semitism not just in the world but also in the Church. I am concerned that Bible-believers do not discern that the devil is real and that we must stand against him. A woman said to me once that if we would leave the devil alone, he would leave us alone!

God give us discernment against every work of the antichrist spirit that is creeping into the Church!

This is by no means a complete list of demonic spirits to deal with, nor a complete description of any of these that I have mentioned. My prayer is that when you discern that something must be put under your feet, you will do the necessary work of studying the characteristics and tactics of any spirit you may discern. The Word of God is rich with insight to identify and pull down every stronghold.

ACTIVATION

As you read this chapter, did any of the descriptions of demonic strongholds open your eyes to something you are currently dealing with in your personal life, ministry or area of influence? Remember, we do not wrestle against flesh and blood but against spiritual forces. If necessary, repent of any alignment, sin, ungodly belief or judgment you have had that has empowered that dark force. Now pray and bind and break the power of that spirit from affecting you and your family. Next write a new decree, proclaiming what God says over you and your situation. Speak this decree out loud as a declaration of your victory.

14

EYES TO SEE,
EARS TO HEAR

And this I pray, that your love may abound still
more and more in knowledge and all discernment,
that you may approve the things that are excellent,
that you may be sincere and without offense till the
day of Christ, being filled with the fruits of righteousness which are by Jesus Christ, to the glory
and praise of God.

Philippians 1:9–11

My husband and I are blessed to have the opportunity
to travel around the world. One of the most interesting New Testament locales we have visited is the ancient ruins
of the city of Ephesus. It is fascinating to realize that it was to
this New Testament apostolic hub that Paul wrote about the
role of the fivefold ministries of apostle, prophet, evangelist,
pastor and teacher, as well as about the armor of God used

for spiritual warfare. The church in this city was established by Paul and was later pastored by his spiritual son, Timothy. It was the place Mary, the mother of Jesus, lived in her later years, as well as the place John, the Revelator, settled after his exile on the Isle of Patmos.

Ephesus was known in the ancient world as the center for training people in magic and the occult arts. It was also a famed city of idolatry, with a massive temple built to honor the goddess Diana (Artemis). Because of this Ephesus was a city that had a strong demonic structure surrounding it. Yet this city also became known for revival and Kingdom transformation. It became the center of Christianity in the world for the next several centuries.

Throughout his letter to the Ephesians, Paul reminded the church that regardless of the evil done in the city, Christ is seated at the right hand of God in heavenly places, "far above all principality and power and might and dominion, and every name that is named, not only in this age but also in that which is to come" (Ephesians 1:21). The dominion of Jesus supersedes the dominion of any demonic structure. God "put all things under His feet, and gave Him to be the head over all things to the church, which is His body, the fullness of Him who fills all in all" (verses 22–23). Paul also told the Ephesians that God has "raised us up together, and made us sit together in the heavenly places in Christ Jesus" (Ephesians 2:6). He went on to reveal God's intention: that "now the manifold wisdom of God might be made known by the church to the principalities and powers in the heavenly places, according to the eternal purpose which He accomplished in Christ Jesus our Lord" (Ephesians 3:10–11).

While on his journeys he wrote to Timothy, encouraging him. Paul used terms like "wage the good warfare," "fight the good fight of faith," "endure hardship as a good soldier," and "no one engaged in warfare entangles himself with the affairs of this life" (1 Timothy 1:18; 6:12; 2 Timothy 2:3–4). He knew for the Kingdom of God to continue to advance in Ephesus, they would have to stay in the spiritual fight.

So it is today. The Church has been directed to declare God's power and wisdom to the principalities and powers in the heavenly places through our actions of demonstrating the Kingdom of God on earth. The Kingdom of heaven is forcefully advancing and forceful men take hold of it (see Matthew 11:12). God has given us everything we need to partner with Him to see His Kingdom come and His will be done on earth as it is in heaven. We are to be the connectors between heaven and earth, by virtue of the power of the risen Christ who will cause the kingdoms of this world to become His kingdoms.

As we clearly discern the move of God's Holy Spirit, His plans and purposes for the earth, the angel armies are fighting for us. As we encounter every demonic foe, we are assured of victory in every endeavor. "Now thanks be to God who always leads us in triumph in Christ" (2 Corinthians 2:14).

A Final Prayer for You, As a Discerner

Lord, I cry out for a deeper level of discernment than ever before. Give me eyes to see and ears to hear in the spirit realm. Sharpen my ability to hear Your voice and to be a watchman on the wall for my family, church, city and nation. Make me as one of the sons of Issachar. Help me to discern the times and strategies, to discern demons and demonic structures. Let me recognize the presence and operation of angels and angel armies and know how to work with them. Help me to be wise as I discern human spirits, and guard my heart from becoming judgmental or critical and from carrying false responsibility. Help me discern Your reformation plans and purposes so I can join the work of Your ekklesia in the earth, bringing Kingdom transformation and life everywhere I go. Anoint me to lead, to build and to war. Give me wisdom as I engage in spiritual battle, recognizing first and foremost that Jesus Christ already defeated every principality and power. Show me my part in the Kingdom so that I can accomplish every spiritual assignment You give me. Your people are on earth to enforce Your victory, extend and expand Your Kingdom and reveal Your glory. Lord, give me a discerning heart so I can stand among those called to "turn the world upside down." In the mighty name of Jesus Christ I pray, Amen!

INDEX

Abaddon, 148
abandonment, 152
Abiathar, 78, 80, 105
Abishag, 79
Abraham, 54–55, 64, 94–95,
    130, 136, 215
Absalom, 78, 79, 89, 90, 175, 236
abundant life, 27
accountability, 173
accusation, 92, 148, 164, 165,
    226, 235
activation, 18, 41
Adam, 37, 150
addiction, 151
Adonijah, 78–79, 89, 90, 105
adultery, 80, 171
adversary, 148
afflict, 232
Africa, 214
agnosticism, 237
Ahab, 228, 231
Ahasuerus, 112
Ahaziah, 232
AIDS, 126

aion, 47–48
air war, 211
Alcorn, Nancy, 91
Alexander I, Czar, 115
alignment, 57, 65–67
Amalekites, 227
ambition, 215, 236
Amorites, 227
anakrino, 35
analogies, 40
Ananias, 130
anapsyxis, 49
angel armies, 23, 132, 139–40,
    183
angelos, 130
angels, 16, 129–44
anger, 152, 162
anointing, 125–26
antichrist spirit, 236–38
anti-Semitism, 238
anxiety, 77
Aphrodite, 231
apokalupsis, 39
Apollyon, 148

apostles, 205–6
Apostles' Creed, 109
Arab Spring, 61
arguments, 164, 234
arrogance, 234
Artaxerxes, 112
Artemis, 231, 240
arts, 222
Ashdod, 203
Ashkelon, 202, 203
Ashtoreth, 85, 228, 231
Astarte, 231
Athaliah, 232
atheism, 237
Athena, 222
authority, 88–90, 111, 113, 155–57, 186–87, 209–10
avarice, 151
awakening, 210–11

Baal, 56, 228, 231, 232
Bailey, Greg, 138
Balaam, 67, 130, 172
Baptists, 105
bar, 225
barrenness, 195
Bathsheba, 78, 80
Battle of Beersheba, 138–39
Battle of Gallipoli, 138
beards, 170
Beatles, 192–93
Beelzebub, 56
Belgium, 203
Belial, 235–36
Benaiah, 78
Bethel Church (Redding, CA), 119
birth, 72
bitterness, 79

blessing, 31, 69, 214, 215
blindness, 195
Body of Christ, 38, 75, 109, 126, 166, 194, 209
Book of Mormon, The, 134
breakthrough, 103, 107, 120, 141, 144
brokenness, 90
Buck, Darrell, 33
business, 95–97

calamity, 151
Caleb, 202
Canaanites, 227
cancer, 155, 212
captivity, 212
"cessation" philosophy, 12
change, 50, 104, 105–6, 209–12
chaos, 225
Chavda, Bonnie, 119
Chavda, Mahesh, 119
China, 165
China Inland Mission, 207
Christian International, 16, 96
Christian International Australia and New Zealand, 138
Christian International Europe, 198
christos, 237
chronos, 47, 48, 50, 55, 56
Church, 104, 156, 204–5, 224, 237, 241
Church of Jesus Christ of Latter-day Saints, 134
cloud, 118
comfort, 162
Communist nations, 165
condemnation, 178
confrontation, 87

confusion, 113, 195–96
constrain, 232
contention, 164, 234
control, 171–72, 211, 229, 230
controversy, 166
Cornelius, 130, 136
corruption, 98, 210, 216–17
courtroom, 185–86
criticism, 17, 36, 162, 173–75
cultural shift, 46
curse, 96
Cyrus, 69, 111–13, 209

dabar shalom, 34–35
Dagon, 203
dance, 124–25
danger, 16
Daniel, 41, 51, 130, 135, 137, 141, 187
Dark Ages, 108
darkness, 16, 61, 103, 185, 210, 224
David, 64, 78, 84, 89–90, 105, 106–7, 137, 149, 203–4, 224, 229, 235, 236
deafness, 195
death, 116–17, 151
Deborah, 64, 229
deception, 19, 37, 227, 228
decrees, 62, 171, 193–95, 213–14, 220
defrauding, 19
delay, 48, 55–57, 113
Delilah, 229
deliverance, 77, 92–93, 136, 141, 146, 154, 158–59
demons, 16, 146–47, 148, 149, 187
  activity of, 151–53
  assignment of, 18–21, 26

attachments of, 92–93
plans of, 213
strongholds of, 147, 151
possession of, 153–55
depression, 152, 232
destiny, 182
destruction, 225
detrimental mindsets, 215–16
diakrino, 35
diakrisis, 35
Diana, 197, 231, 240
diligence, 85
disappointment, 195–96
discerning of spirits, 36
discernment
  activation of, 18
  of angels, 129–44
  as clouded, 171–73
  definition of, 36
  and faith, 14
  of hearts, 82–84
  in reformation, 108–10
  of Solomon, 81–82, 84–86, 105–7
  and spiritual warfare, 181–99
  war over, 12–14
  vs. wisdom, 37–38
discriminate, 36
diseases, 195
disobedience, 57
disruptors, 110–13
divination, 232–33
divine reversal, 194–95
division, 19, 102, 165, 227
doctrine, 134
dominion, 183–84, 240
donkeys, 68, 130, 172
"double portion" anointing, 45
doubt, 196
downfalls, 85

doxa, 120
dreams, 36, 40, 83–84, 95, 103, 158, 169
drought, 52–54
dunamis, 28, 186–87, 192

economic recession, 44–45, 65
edification, 162, 178
Edwards, Gene, 90
Eivaz, Jennifer, 236
ekklesia, 104, 204–5, 207, 210–11, 219
Ekron, 203
Eliab, 169
Elijah, 53, 141–42, 228, 229
Elisha, 131–32
Elizabeth, 135
emotions, 132, 146, 170
enemies, 175
England, 204
enlightened, 217
envy, 152
Ephesus, 217, 239–40
"epidemic revival," 46
epiginosko, 167
equality, 215
Esther, 193–94, 229
eternity, 48
evangelist, 206
Eve, 37, 150
evil, and good, 12, 33, 37–38
exhortation, 162
exousia, 186–87
Ezekiel, 195, 198, 208

faith, 14, 28, 54, 55
faking, 122–23
false brothers, 164–66, 180
false doctrine, 134
false prophets, 114, 227

false religions, 237
false responsibility, 175–76
famine, 45
fear, 77, 117, 152, 158–59, 170, 196, 227
feelings, 17, 146, 170–71
fertility, 231
Florida, 43, 52–54, 96, 181, 214, 216
forgotten, 196
foundations, 101–2, 108, 110
Four Horsemen of Awakening and Revival, 138
France, 203–4
freedom, 93
fruit, 179

Gabriel, 134, 135, 137, 187
Gad, 182
Gamaliel, 121
Gath, 203–4
Gay, Robert, 185–86
Gaza, 204
gender, 238
Germany, 203
Gideon, 44, 136
Girgashites, 227
Gladwell, Malcom, 60
Glasgow, Scotland, 214
God
    glory of, 118–20, 144
    mood of, 120
    move of, 121–23
    nature of, 150
    presence of, 116–17
    voice of, 22, 29–31, 76, 127, 149–50, 172
"going behind the veil," 19
Goll, James, 30
good, and evil, 12, 33, 37–38

gossip, 17, 179
government, 97–99
greed, 84, 151
Greek mythology, 222
grief, 152, 235
ground war, 211–12
guarding, 83–84, 86
Guatemala, 216
gut reaction, 16, 123, 126, 146, 174

Hagar, 130, 136
Haggai, 113
Hamon, Bill, 16, 17, 18, 19, 66, 94, 96, 98, 109–10, 127, 157, 158, 169, 171, 173, 189–90, 198–99
Hamon, Evelyn, 16, 96–97
Hamon, Tom, 11, 25, 44, 56, 76–77, 88, 103, 126, 142, 151, 158, 162, 171, 173, 178, 205–6, 216
hardness of heart, 77
healing, 33, 35, 54, 76, 194–95, 212
hearing, 30–31, 34–35, 41
hearts, 82–84
Hebron, 224
Henderson, Lacelia, 12–13
Herodias, 229
Hezekiah, 66, 138
Hiram of Tyre, King, 96
Hittites, 227
Hivites, 227
Holy Spirit
  gifts of, 15, 35, 75
  mood of, 120
  outpouring of, 28, 71, 121
  power of, 156, 186
  presence of, 116

homosexuality, 126
honor, 89
hopelessness, 229
hora, 50–52, 54
hosts, 139
house cleaning, 76–77
humanism, 148, 203, 237
humiliation, 227
humility, 67, 68, 102, 172, 173, 235
hurricane, 213
hurt, 90

ideologies, 211
idolatry, 57, 66, 84, 203, 231
imitation, 125
immorality, 126, 151
independence, 235
infirmity, 152
influence, 87, 102, 178, 197
injustice, 223
insanity, 152
intellectual awareness, 113–14
intercession, 67–68, 93, 207–9
Ishmael, 55
Ishtar, 231
ISIS, 61, 199
Islam, 134, 139, 165
Issachar, 62–63
"Issachar Anointing," 45, 59–73

Jacob, 67, 69, 130, 142, 229
Jacobs, Cindy, 63
Jante Law, 215–16
jealousy, 152
Jebusites, 227
Jehoiada, 232
Jeremiah, 98
Jeshua, 112
Jesse, 169

Jesus Christ
blood of, 159, 190–91
Body of, 38, 75, 109, 126, 166, 194, 209
building his Church, 107–8
discernment of, 166–68
as manifestation of God's *Shekinah*, 119
on signs of the times, 45–47
victory on the cross, 184
Jezebel spirit, 170, 175, 221–22, 226, 228–31
Joab, 78, 79–80, 105
Joash, 232
Johnson, Bill, 119
John the Baptist, 130, 135, 229
John the Revelator, 130, 133, 240
Joseph, 41, 44, 54, 55, 94
Joshua, 130, 169, 202
joy, 72, 235
Jubilee year, 139
Judaizers, 237
judgmentalism, 17, 36, 92, 162, 164, 173–75
Jungle Book, The, 233
junk, 76–77
justice, 175, 223

kabowd, 118
kairos, 47, 48–50, 51, 54–55, 69, 136
katanoeo, 168
katischyo, 108
Kingdom of God, 22, 66, 99, 102, 104–5, 127, 157, 166, 183–84, 197, 199, 205, 214, 240–41
knowledge, 63
koakh, 29, 197
krino, 35
kritikos, 163

Laban, 142, 229
laughter, 123
Law, 66
lawless action, 151
Law of Jante, 215
leaders, 40–41, 64–65, 66, 73, 87–99, 167–68, 209–10
Leah, 69–70, 71
LeClaire, Jennifer, 188
Leviathan, 56, 232–35
lies, 17, 148
Light Horsemen, 138–39
limitation, 215–16
listening, 34–35, 41, 81–82
Little Mermaid, 230
logos, 66
Lord of hosts, 139
love, 163, 174–75
Lucifer, 132, 135, 149
Lutherans, 105
Luther, Martin, 109
Lydia, 218

Makkedah, 169
malak, 130
man, nature of, 150–51
Managua, Nicaragua, 213
mandrakes, 70
manipulation, 229, 230
marriage, 173–74
Mary (mother of Jesus), 51, 130, 135, 240
Maxwell, John, 87
Meni, 182
mercy, 174–75
Mercy Multiplied, 91
messenger, 135–37
methodeia, 184
Methodists, 105
Michael, 135, 137, 139, 187

Milcom, 85
mind, 83, 170
mindsets, 215–16
ministering angels, 141–43
miphtan, 233
miracles, 54, 125, 127, 143
Mohammed, 134
Molech, 85
Mordecai, 193
Mormon church, 134
Moroni, 134
Moses, 117–18, 119, 130, 136,
   198
mountains, 65–66
mourning, 234
murder, 80
Murillo, Rosario, 213
music, 192–93
Muslim Brotherhood, 61

Naboth, 235
nachash, 234–35
nakar, 114
names, 224–26
Nashville, 221–23, 230
Nathan, 78
nations, 209–12
natsar, 208
natural realm, 18, 27
natural resources, 214
natural senses, 32, 33, 40
Nee, Watchman, 30
Nehemiah, 113–14
Netherlands, 201–2
new governance, 212
new season, 104, 105, 109
"new thing," 111
Nicaragua, 213
Nigeria, 199
Norway, 215

obedience, 30–31, 86, 218
occult, 148, 165
oikodomeo, 108
open visions, 32, 202
ophis, 156
oppression, 19, 60, 93, 151, 212,
   227, 232
"out of the box," 119, 122
outpouring, 121–22, 126

pain, 33, 71, 232
panhandle, of Florida, 43,
   52–54, 96, 181
paradigm shift, 111
Parkes, Bob, 153
Parkes, Sharon, 153–55
Parthenon, 222
passivity, 57
Patton, George, 191
Paul, 83, 110, 130, 132, 137,
   152–53, 156, 165, 166, 173,
   184, 188, 195, 197, 217–18,
   239–40
peace, 34–35, 144, 196–97
Pentecost, 71, 143
Pentecostals, 105
perceive, 114, 167
Peretti, Frank, 20
Perizzites, 103, 227
persecution, 61, 105, 188–89,
   195
perseverance, 71
personality, 174
perversion, 151, 203
Peter, 49, 130, 136
pethen, 233
Pharisees, 168
Philippines, 98–99
Philistines, 203

Phillip, 136, 212
photizo, 217
phroureo, 83
Pierce, Chuck, 11–14, 51–52, 65, 182
pillar of fire, 118
"ping," 123, 124
polytheism, 237
poverty, 152, 181–83, 197, 214
power, 28, 186–87
praise, 192–93
prayer, 40, 62, 81–82, 131, 177, 178–79, 191–92, 208–9
prejudice, 152, 171, 238
prevail, 108
pride, 56, 83, 90, 152, 172, 234, 235, 236
prince of Persia, 137, 187
proclamations, 193–95
propaganda, 211
prophecy, 27–29, 36, 62, 195–96, 198–99, 230
prosperity, 25, 31, 43–44, 63–64, 68–69, 95–96, 127, 142, 197–98, 214
protection, 141, 158
Protestant Reformation, 105, 109, 139
punching, 198–99
Python spirit, 221–22, 226, 232–35

Queen of Heaven, 231–32

Rabshakeh, 225–26
race, 238
Rachel, 69–70, 71
rage, 152, 164–65
Rahab, 225
Rahabar, 225

rain, 52–54
Ramos, Fidel, 98
real estate, 63–64, 182
rebellion, 36, 79, 152
red flags, 164
reformation, 66, 104, 108–10
refreshing, 49
rejection, 152
religious spirit, 104–5, 121
Renner, Rick, 39
repentance, 57, 77, 93, 96, 102, 125, 159, 203, 231, 238
resistance, 113
responsibility, 21, 81, 88, 175–76, 177, 178
restoration, 66, 91, 125, 160
retaliation, 157
revelation, 36–40, 173
reversal, 194–95
revival, 46, 49, 72, 98, 103, 116, 126
revolution, 192–93
rewards, 69–71
rhema, 66
Rio de Janiero, Brazil, 145–46
robbery, 25–27, 33, 216
Roman Catholics, 105, 109
Rome, 205

sacrifices, 112
Samson, 68, 136, 229
Samuel, 169
Sarah, 54–55, 136
Satan, 132, 134, 147–52, 153, 156, 157, 184, 190–91, 197, 228
Satanism, 88
Saul, 89–90, 99, 229
Scotland, 214
Scripture. *See* Word

seasons, 48
selfishness, 83
Sennacherib, 226
senses, 31–34
sensuality, 123, 124
sex-trafficking, 216
sexual abuse, 170
sexual immorality, 151, 163, 229
shalom, 34–35, 106
shama, 34, 41, 81
shamar, 208
shame, 195–96, 227
Sheets, Dutch, 50, 208
Sheets, Tim, 140
Shekinah, 117, 119
shouting, 198–99
sickness, 152
Signs and Wonders Conference, 119
signs of the times, 45–47
Silas, 130, 217–18
sin, 84, 150, 152, 159, 183, 229
skepticism, 237
slanderer, 148
Smith, Joseph, 134
snake, 176
"snake handling," 156
snakes, 233
Solomon, 78–79, 80–82, 84–86, 88–89, 90, 96, 97, 99, 105–7, 118
soul, 17, 125, 169–71
South America, 214
"spirit of Egypt," 60
spirit of resistance, 113, 114
spirit of robbery, 25–27, 33, 216
spirit realm, 18, 27, 36, 38, 131–32, 148, 178
spiritual authority, 88–90

spiritual DNA, 183
spiritual foundation, 102
spiritual senses, 32
spiritual slumber, 57
spiritual warfare, 19, 181–99, 208–9, 219, 224–25
Spurgeon, Charles, 79
Stark, David, 214
Stark, Emma, 214
St. Isaac's Cathedral, 115
Stone, Sharon, 198
stranglehold, 188
strategy, 217–18
strife, 152, 234
strongholds, 219, 221–38
stubbornness, 234
students, 41
submission, 235
symbols, 40

Tamar, 236
Taylor, J. Hudson, 207
Temple, 106, 107, 111–12, 113, 118
Ten Commandments, 117
territorial transformation, 147, 182–83, 197, 201–20
testing the spirits, 123–25
tet, 72
thief, 27
Third Great Awakening, 46, 72, 140
Third Reformation, 109–10
threshold, 233
time, 47–52, 218–19
Timothy, 195, 240
tipping-point moment, 60–62
Tokamene, 20–21, 225
Tola, 64

tongues, 143–44, 191
Torah, 62
traits, 73
transformation, 98
transition, 104, 111
traps, 114
Tree of the Knowledge of Good
and Evil, 37
tribulation, 236
trigger, 170
tsaba, 139
tsaphah, 208
tyranny, 151

unbelief, 196
unforgiveness, 77, 152
unity, 102, 209
universalism, 237
unrighteous decrees, 213–14
unseen realm, 131–32
Ursula, 230

victory, 85, 152, 159, 185, 196,
230
vigilant, 208
violence, 151
visions, 36, 40, 202, 230
voice, of God, 149–50, 172
voodoo, 145–46

Wagner, C. Peter, 109
war, 149

war council, 211
warrior angels, 137–39
watchman, 18, 67, 163, 207–9
wealth, 69, 182, 197–98
weapons, 189–99
weather patterns, 65
Welsh revival, 202
"why" behind the "what,"
91–92
wiles, 184
will, 170
wisdom, 22, 23, 37–38, 81, 173
witchcraft, 93, 147, 165, 198, 213
wolf, 175, 176
women, 229
Word, 12, 40, 47, 109, 123, 127,
132, 134, 144, 163, 190
World War I, 138
World War II, 191
worship, 54, 120, 131, 133, 161,
192–93
wrestling, 188

X-ray, 38

yada, 63

Zacharias, 130, 135
Zadok, 78
Zebulun, 65
Zechariah, 113, 130
Zerubbabel, 112

Jane Hamon serves, with her husband, Tom, as senior pastor of Vision Church @ Christian International. In their more than 38 years of ministry together, they have built a thriving local church, ministered in more than sixty nations, and helped lead Christian International Ministries, founded by Dr. Bill Hamon. A clear prophetic voice and eloquent teacher, Jane travels extensively ministering at national and international conferences, consulting with leaders, conducting prophetic workshops and teaching at Bible colleges. She is featured frequently on a variety of Christian television programs. A gifted storyteller, she sprinkled her three former books—*Dreams and Visions* (Chosen, 2016), *The Deborah Company* (Destiny Image, 2007) and *The Cyrus Decree* (Christian International, 2001)—with rich personal experiences, extensive research and valuable teaching. Jane attended Christ for the Nations Institute in Dallas, Texas, and later received a bachelor of theology and an honorary doctorate of divinity from Christian International School of Theology.

Jane makes her home in beautiful Santa Rosa Beach, Florida, where she enjoys fulfilling some of her favorite roles in life as wife, mother and now "Mimi" to her growing number of grandchildren.

For further information, please contact Jane at:
www.facebook.com/ApostleJaneHamon
visionchurchci.org
Christianinternational.com
Instagram.com/tomandjanehamon

More from Jane Hamon

Does God still speak through dreams and visions today? Absolutely, says Jane Hamon. In this updated edition of her bestselling book, Hamon unravels the scriptural meanings of dreams and visions and offers a 10-step process for interpretation. Learn the language God is using to show you His purposes for your life.

Dreams and Visions

Stay up to date on your favorite books and authors with our free e-newsletters. Sign up today at chosenbooks.com.

facebook.com/chosenbooks

@chosen_books

@Chosen_Books

Made in the USA
Las Vegas, NV
25 October 2021